Stories
of
Falling Toward Grace

Stories

of

Falling Toward Grace

by
Carlton Allen

Smyth & Helwys Publishing, Inc.®
Macon, Georgia

ISBN 1-880837-81-1

Stories of Falling Toward Grace
by
Carlton Allen

Printed in the United States of America

The paper used in this publication meets the minimum
requirements of American Standard for Information Sciences
—Permanence of paper for Printed Library Materials,
ANSI Z39.48–1984.

Library of Congress Cataloging-in-Publication Data

Allen, Carlton
    Stories of falling toward grace / Carlton Allen.
    viii + 124 pp.   6" x 9" (15 x 23 cm.)
    ISBN 1-880837-81-1
    1. Christian life. 2. Conduct of life. 3. Grace (Theology)
    I. Title.
    BV4501.2.A393   1995
    248.4—dc20   94-28529
                                                CIP

Cover photo compliments of Margaret Mohr, Bloomington, Indiana. Photographer, Serletia Garrett Sims; Cateechee, South Carolina, July 1955.

Contents

For my father
who taught me the meaning of grace

Acknowledgments

The publication of these stories is, in itself, a story of grace. Many people have been gracious in giving of themselves and their time. Though fearful of neglecting some persons who are deserving, I feel I must take this opportunity to thank a few in particular.

Carolyn Zeigler, Jim Pitts, and the late Jim Bowers have at various time and in their own gifted ways both challenged and encouraged me to develop and use my own gifts. Each of these persons has been both friend and mentor, and my life has been enriched by their presence.

I shall always count it a sign of God's grace that I have had the privilege of growing up in Wrens, Georgia; being educated at Furman University; and serving the people of the First Baptist Church of Greenwood, South Carolina. I also know that such opportunities might not have been afforded me were it not for the loving sacrifice of my mother, Louise Dodd Allen.

During the time these stories were written, the church was graciously served by six skillful secretaries. I offer my gratitude to Janelle Anderson, Ann Ella Dorn, Joyce Williams, Lois Grice, Grace Burton, and Nell Morton for their patient and able assistance in translating my scribbles to computer disk.

Finally, I am indebted to my wife, Donna, and our children, Elizabeth, Vicki and Carl, for all the laughter, patience, and love they have so graciously given me. How wonderful to fall into their embrace at the end of each day!

Carlton Allen
Greenwood, South Carolina
February, 1994

Lord is it possible to fall toward grace?
Could I be moved to believe in new beginnings?
Can I be moved?

David Bottoms
"In a U-Haul North of Damascus"

Falling
Toward
Grace

At least the night was perfect for baseball, even if my plans had been less than that. I had ordered tickets for the game six weeks before—not because I wanted to see the Braves play the Giants, but because I found out I would have to be in Atlanta for a meeting. I drove up from Augusta in the morning, and the meeting was completed by 4:00 P.M. To that point, things went well. In fact, I was beginning to think destiny was with me.

When I ordered the tickets, I had no idea the Braves would be trying to clinch their second straight division championship on the night I would attend. I bought two tickets and invited my college roommate to join me for the game. He was an attorney in Atlanta, and we had not seen each other in a year. Family and business had encroached upon the bonds of brotherhood and sports and the shared struggle of surviving college. Both of us had freely made our choices, and I think David was as happy as I was. Still, the few times we did manage to get together were wonderful. I experienced a sense of freedom and acceptance when we were together that I did not have at work nor at home now that children were present. We did not need this time together more than once or twice a year, but skipping a year created an intense longing for the experience.

The game was a rare opportunity. I was approaching the burn-out stage at work, a cyclical status that simply came with the territory. I had a long list of stories and jokes I needed to share with David and, judging from our too few phone conversations, he was in about the same predicament. We were both loyal Braves fans, and the chance to be at the game together, when the Braves might clinch the division title, would be icing on the cake. Speaking of icing, the seats would be sweet as well: aisle seats twenty rows behind the outfield end of the third-base dugout—unbelievable!

Perhaps I should have realized this situation was all too good. After my meeting, I drove to David's office. He was leaving to meet with a client who had called out of the blue—something about tax evasion. I understood; but we both hated the situation. He had made reservations at a good restaurant, Houston's, and insisted I go on there. He told me the safest place to sell my extra ticket to the scalpers and was gone. I could have called a couple of other people, but I was afraid my disappointment would make me poor company for anyone.

I had a great steak at Houston's and arrived at the stadium early. The ten dollar ticket sold for fifty dollars within five minutes. David had said I could get a hundred if I was patient, but I was not greedy, nor was I in the mood to take such a risk. I knew that the guy who bought it would probably sell it for around a hundred dollars, but I preferred letting him wander around the parking lot looking over his shoulder for the police while I settled in to watch the end of batting practice.

The only problem with selling a ticket in the lot is that you never know who will sit beside you. Fifteen minutes before the start of the game, I glanced to my left and saw a dingy pair of running shoes that gave me my first hint. The dirty canvas of the shoes was broken by bright orange stripes. The shoes were the kind worn by people who never do any running. (I always wonder why such people buy those shoes. Do they plan to run but just do not get around to it? Do they really think they are fooling anyone? Surely they do not buy them for looks, and other shoes are certainly more comfortable.)

As my eyes continued upwards, I caught a glimpse of black socks and—a couple of inches above the ankle—the beginning (or should I say end) of a pair of camouflage pants. The pants were brown, green, and tan and baggy and stained at the knees. The tight, black tee-shirt was a contrast to the pants. An ample belly and waistline provided the tension for the fabric. On the front of the shirt was an eerie splotch of yellow, white, and red—maybe a rock group's emblem.

Finally my gaze reached the face that was half shielded by a Braves' cap. I saw curls of hair protruding from the sides and behind the neck. The hair was a reddish-brown color, but a little too dingy for auburn. The face bore a moustache that was even redder—not at all a match for the curls that seemed to erupt from beneath the cap. The moustache was elongated by a rather dopey grin—not a smile, just a half-witted grin.

"Scuse me, buddy," he said as he moved sideways in the row. I turned my knees into the aisle to allow more room, yet I was still brushed by a canvas sport-bag slung over his shoulder. I kept my mouth shut, though, not really caring to engage in conversation. At first he looked farther down the row, and my hopes soared. Then he glanced at his ticket stub, holding it near the back of the seat as if he could not read the numbers and had to rely on matching the curves and angles on the ticket stub and seat-back in order to determine if he was in the right place.

Eventually he muttered, "Yep," then smiled, dropped his bag, and settled into the seat beside me. I leaned closer to the aisle, hoping this would discourage him from trying to talk to me. Yet, I could not help glancing at him out of the corner of my eye. I was fascinated by the mismatched outfit.

"Hey, Blackhawks," he said, pointing his thumb up and smiling as he nodded his head. At first I thought he was nuts, then I saw a guy in a Chicago Blackhawks hockey jersey standing five rows down from us. The guy in the jersey looked at him but did not smile, nod, or gesture; he did not acknowledge this grinning idiot. I felt sorry for the man next to me, but still did not want to talk to him. He still smiled and nodded his head as if the jerk in the jersey had not just snubbed him in front of a dozen or more people. I was embarrassed that I had been so repulsed by his appearance.

"Cold beer, right here!" the vendor shouted. I jumped as though shot. I had been so busy watching the guy I had not seen the beer man coming. The guy became a blur of fumbling hands and canvas as he searched for a side pocket on the sports bag. He pulled out two bills and reached over me saying, "Right here, right here." The beer man took the money and began pouring the drink. The guy nudged my shoulder and said, "Better get one now, buddy."

"No thanks," I muttered, watching as he reached over me to grasp the cup even before the vendor had finished pouring. My fears were realized as he jostled the cup, spilling drops of beer on the cuff of my trousers and my shoe.

"Oh, sorry," he said, then adding with that half-witted grin, "might as well have one now; the ol' lady's gonna' smell it on you anyway."

My sympathy quickly dissipated as I shifted to turn from him without making a reply. About that time the national anthem was sung by a vocal ensemble from Morehouse College. The singers were exceptional, but I could concentrate on the beauty of their tone for only a moment, for I was distracted by my neighbor. He took off his cap and held it over his chest, but kept turning from side to side looking at the crowd while he half-sang and half-hummed with the ensemble. I managed to avoid eye-contact and tried to focus on the game as we again sat.

From the corner of my eye, I could see my neighbor pull something large and yellow from his canvas bag. As he rustled paper, I took a better look and saw a twelve-inch sub sandwich. It was spilling over with thin slices of meat, cheese, and tomatoes and shredded lettuce and onions. I was amazed to see him stuff the end in his mouth, wiggling it back and forth before biting and tearing off the end. Strings of lettuce trailed from his mouth, dripping with the oily dressing. He used one hand to stuff the excess into his mouth, then began chewing with an annoying, loud smacking noise.

Watching him eat the sandwich was disgusting, but I could not stop. I could not believe his capacity for getting his mouth around the entire stack of bread, meat, cheese, and condiments. At one point a large blob of oily mayonnaise dropped into his lap. He used the waxy paper in which the sandwich was wrapped to wipe it off, then licked the excess from his fingers. I have no idea why we are transfixed by that which disgusts us—by that which we abhor—but the fact is undeniable. Perhaps my disgust fed my need to feel superior to someone else. Perhaps I was curious to see someone do that which I had obviously been taught was taboo. In some sense, I felt like a voyeur—one who takes great pleasure from secretly watching another. My pleasure was heightened rather than diminished by the guilt that accompanied it.

I was distracted by the crowd as some persons stood and the noise level rose. One of the Braves had hit a ball to the warning track. I had lost track of the batting order, and the ball was caught against the wall anyway. I realized I was getting angry at this situation. I could not understand why.

As I settled back into my seat, I noticed, with relief, that the man next to me was wrapping the rest of the sandwich. As he put the remains back into his sports-bag, he let out a loud belch. He never looked up or around; he had no sense of shame or embarrassment. I was no longer able to sit there. I went to the concession stand and returned with a coke and some peanuts.

The guy watched me as I sat down once again. I could feel his eyes on me. I tried desperately not to look in his direction, but I was like a moth drawn to a car's headlights. When I did glance to the side, he was staring right at me. I wondered how long he would have stared. He looked at my cup and said, "I told you you should have gotten your beer when the vendor was here."

I tried to smile as I said, "Well, this is a Coke."

"Just as well," he said as he got out of his seat, "I mean, you know what they say, 'You don't buy beer; you just rent it.' " With that, he pushed by me into the aisle.

In years past I could have moved to any number of other seats while he was gone. This year, however, each game had been packed, and with the possibility of Atlanta clinching the division title that night there was no empty seat in the stadium. I realized at this point that I had pretty much lost track of the game, which further angered me.

As I looked out to the field I saw that the Braves had a runner on first base. I had no idea how he had gotten there. Two pitches later he stole second base on a close play. Then with the count two and two, the batter hit a sinking liner to the gap in right-center field. The ball touched ground just beyond the out-stretched glove of the diving Giants' center-fielder. As the ball rolled to the wall, the runner rounded third and headed for home. The batter tried to stretch the sure double into a triple. He and the ball arrived at third at the same instant, but he slid hard, knocking the ball from the third baseman's grasp.

On the very next pitch, with the crowd still in a frenzy, the batter ripped a line drive over the third-base bag. The third baseman speared it with a brilliant back-handed dive then, twisting in the air as he came down, managed to catch the corner of the bag with his foot to double the runner off third. The inning was over with a play that I knew would be in every highlight film at the end of the week.

"What happened? What happened?" My neighbor was back, stepping on my feet as he watched the field while trying to get to his seat. He missed everything but the crowd's roars.

I think at that instant I realized this was the story of this guy's life. He probably attended twenty or thirty games a season, and yet the most exciting and crucial plays of the season found him in the bathroom. I lucked into seeing the big event of the only game I would see the whole year, and he had to rely on my description to know what happened. My feeling of pity returned. I recounted the sequence of events as best I could. He stared wide-eyed, taking it all in, reminding me of my six year-old son when I would read him a scary story out of one of his favorite books.

When I finished my account of the play, he shook his head. "Man," he said, "I can't believe I missed that. You know I live out in Conyers, so I get here ten or twelve times a season. Came up tonight with no ticket but figgered I could find one. Scalpers'll make a killin' tonight but, hey, some things you just gotta do."

I managed a smile and asked his occupation. I could not believe I was starting this conversation, but found myself unable to cut it off.

"Me, oh I run a forklift at a plant. Been with 'em twelve years now—sorta' worked my way up to a 'sit-down job'," he said. "What about you?"

"I work with a bank in Augusta," I said, trying to glance back at the field in the hope he would again become interested in the game.

"Banker, eh?" he said with a grin that unnerved me. "My wife worked at a bank the summer after she got out of high school. Mighta' made a career outta' it iffen' she hadn't had to quit to have the baby."

I knew I did not want to hear more details at this point, but I could not stop him.

"Yep, I got her pregnant. Shouldn't 'a done it, I know, but she was a hot little thang. Did right by her, though. We got married that fall. Kid's fifteen now an' we got three more. Lou Ann works at Wal-Mart now—ain't a bad job at all."

I had no idea what to say. Actually I thought it incredulous that someone would tell such a story to a total stranger. All I could manage to utter was, "Well, as long as you're happy." I regretted those words as soon as they came out of my mouth.

"Yeah, I s'pose so," he drawled. "I guess you could say we's happy. Lou Ann gets on to me now an,' then but I reckon that's what wives is s'posed to do. Last time I came to a game—last month, it was—she got upset at me. Can't blame her though. I left here an' went by the Bare Essence Lounge, that strip joint offa' I-20. You ever been there?"

"No," I said, trying not to sound sanctimonious. I heard the beer vendor behind me and said, "Think I'll get one now."

"Yeah, yeah; me too, me too," the man next to me said, as he began fumbling again with his canvas bag.

I hoped the interruption would get him off-track, but he continued, "Got drunk that night an' knew I couldn't make it home, so I got a room at Motel 6 an' slept it off. Lou Ann had got scairt that I'd wrecked or somethin' and had called the police so I had ta' tell her the truth. I guess it ain't the first time I screwed up, but she's a good woman an' she knows I don't mean nothin'; an' I bring home a decent check for her an' them kids. 'Course I was late for work that day, too, an' my boss threatened to fire me, but he's a good fella' too." He drained his cup of beer—mine was still half-full—and stood. "You ready for another? It's on me, buddy."

"No,"I said, "I've still got a good bit in here."

He pushed by me into the aisle, and I tried to concentrate on the game but could not. I had dealt with hundreds like him in my work. They wanted loans to finance their dreams, but I could tell from their history and personality it would not work. Yet, I could never convince them that I was doing them a favor by turning down their loan application. I do not know if it was child-like innocence, stupidity, or a stubborn streak, but they usually became angry with me because they refused to believe they would fail. Most of those persons would eventually obtain their loans but lose all they had as a result of non-payment, ruined because they finally found a banker they could snooker or who did not care if the loan went bad as long as the bank could collect enough on the collateral. There are snakes in every profession.

I knew this guy's type. I knew that his marriage was probably crumbling, his job was probably hanging by a thread, and he was most likely oblivious to all of this. I could not understand why he fascinated me. I dreaded, virtually hated, his type. Was it because of my training? As a banker, I quickly learned that bad risks had to be identified. Compassion was just a quick way to end two careers—the loan applicant's and mine.

I remembered that David once told me about a lawyer he had faced. The guy was ruthless—at times willing to stretch, if not outright break the rules to win. David said the man fascinated him because he could see a bit of himself in this cold-hearted, ambition-driven person. David would never have employed this man's tactics and, in fact, was good enough not to need them, yet he followed the man's career as we did our favorite Brave's statistics.

Was I seeing something of myself in this forklift driver? But what? My marriage was solid; his was falling apart. Jan and I had not married out of high school, nor had I gotten her pregnant then. I certainly was not in danger of losing my job. I loved my work and was good at it. Of course, a lot of banks had failed recently, and others had undergone major changes due to mergers and buyouts, but I felt my bank was pretty solid. Even if we were bought out, surely I would be retained.

The roar of the crowd again interrupted my thought. There was another long fly. This time it carried—a three-run homer. The Braves were ahead 6-2 in the sixth inning. The guy returned and, again, I filled him in on what he had missed.

"They're gonna' do it," he said as he pumped his right fist into the air. "Back to back, man, and this time I bet they go all the way." He glanced behind him and almost fell over the back of his seat. "Hey, the guy from Roswell, how ya' doin'?"

He struck up a conversation with a couple behind us, a conversation that was decidedly one-sided. The couple barely responded to anything he said. A couple of times I noticed, when he was not looking, that they rolled their eyes and shook their heads to one another.

My thoughts drifted again to what David had said, but there was no part of me in this guy. We were so different, and yet I wondered if it was because I made good choices and he did not. Could one decision either way have changed either of our lives? What if he had resisted his sexual urges as a teenager? What if I given in more to mine? Was it one decision, or did each decision lead to another—like being lost and constantly changing direction, thinking that each new trail has to be the one that will lead to safety?

The game was down to the final three outs. Everyone was standing, poised to celebrate. If someone had not stood, the thick sense of anticipation would have drawn that person bodily from the seat. Mounted policeman suddenly appeared on the field. I knew each person felt as I did—as if we were there on the field. We were experiencing the vicarious excitement that comes only from a dramatic moment in sports.

"Listen," he said, "this place is gonna' go nuts when they win. The whole city'll be like that—I know from last year. Places like the Bare Essence will really be jumpin'—you gotta' join me. We can swing by for an hour or two."

I was so caught up in the excitement of the crowd that I was afraid for a moment that I had said, "Yes." Then I turned to him and grabbed his arm. I had to pull him closer to be heard. "No, I can't. I . . . I mean I'd better not. But, you'd better not either. What about your wife and work?"

"Oh, I'll only be an hour or so," he said, yelling as the Braves got their second out.

"Yeah, right," I said and forcibly turned him to look him in the eye.

We never saw the third out. We looked at one another until he finally said, "Hey, you're right. I go there, I get caught up in the party, and who knows what could happen."

"Go home," I said. "Do the right thing again."

Out on I-20 I was still thinking about how close I had come to saying, "Yes. Yeah, I'll go to the strip club. Yes, I'll take a chance on throwing it all away for beer and naked flesh." Of course, I probably could have gotten away with it, but it scared me to think that one decision could have led to others and those to still others.

Even though I had made some bad choices of my own at times—not this time. I had helped someone make the right choice for a change.

I heard a car horn and checked my rear-view mirror. There was a car behind me, but too far back to be angry at my speed. The horn sounded again, and I glanced to my right. He was there in an old pickup truck, grinning and giving me the thumbs-up sign, just as he had the guy in the Blackhawks jersey. I smiled and waved back, just as he pulled onto the exit ramp. I changed lanes and accelerated. As I did, I glanced in the mirror. There, off to the right, against the blackness of a starless night was the pink neon sign of the Bare Essence Lounge.

I remembered a poem by an Atlantan, David Bottoms, in which he wondered if it were possible to "fall toward grace." I think I probably have, and I hoped this guy could, too.

The Gifts
of the
Craftsman

Years ago in the hills of North Carolina lived a gentle old man named Seth. Seth was a lover of music and an accomplished craftsman, a skill that led him to become a maker of dulcimers. People throughout the hills owned Seth's instruments, which were noted for the gracefulness of their design and the haunting beauty of their sound.

Seth lived alone high on a hill, somewhat isolated from others. He had always preferred the sound of the mockingbirds to that of people. In fact, Seth's primary contact with the outside world were his helpers, Matthew and Jonas, two teen-aged boys who went to Seth's cabin twice a week to help with chores and bring mail and groceries from the village in the valley below.

Matthew secured the job for the two boys. As long as he could remember, Matthew's grandmother had played one of Seth's dulcimers, one of the first that Seth had made. Matthew always enjoyed winter evenings by the fire when his grandmother would sit in her rocker, gently caressing the strings as the deep grained wood of the instrument glowed warmly with the light of the fire. Sometimes she would sing hymns; other times she would softly hum.

Over the years Matthew developed a fascination for Seth's instruments, so when he heard that the old man was looking for help he went to see him. The job was more than one boy his age could do, so Matthew talked his best friend, Jonas, into joining him—even though Jonas preferred to spend his time hunting and fishing.

Matthew always saw to it that Jonas did the outside work, which suited Jonas fine. Matthew had the task of cleaning Seth's work area, where the dulcimers were. Matthew took great care in cleaning the completed instruments and handling the ones Seth was still forming.

The diligence with which each boy performed his assigned tasks impressed Seth from the beginning, and soon he developed a deep affection for his two helpers. The work the boys did was invaluable to the craftsman, given his age and condition, and certainly allowed him more time to craft his instruments; but Seth was not able to pay them what he would have liked. Because he took so much time in perfecting each instrument and yet refused to ask more than a modest sum for each, Seth was not a man of wealth. These thoughts burdened the kind gentleman for a couple of years before he finally seized upon an idea that would allow him to show his appreciation to the boys.

Matthew wondered why a padlock suddenly appeared on one of Seth's cabinets. For months, each time he started to clean, the cabinet was secured, and Seth gave no indication that it ought to be opened. Matthew wondered, but had been raised to respect the privacy of others and thus never pursued the matter.

Then one day, as the boys entered the cabin, Seth met them with a sense of urgency and excitement in his voice. Quickly he led them to his work area where they spotted two beautiful matched dulcimers on a table. They were Seth's gifts to the boys. Matthew was awed by the gesture. The beautifully intricate details of the carving had obviously taken hours of painstaking work. Each instrument shone with a dark, rich luster that highlighted the grain of the wood. Delicately smooth to the touch and yet solidly put together, Matthew realized the dulcimers were even more beautiful than his grandmother's.

Though touched by the old man's loving gift, Jonas was not as awe-struck as Matthew. Quickly and awkwardly, he strummed the strings a couple of times, graciously thanked Seth, and left to begin his work. After a few minutes of carefully examining his gift and softly playing part of a simple tune, Matthew stammered his heartfelt gratitude and gently set aside the dulcimer to begin his work —which was frequently interrupted that day as he found himself pausing to stare at his new treasure.

The weeks and months ahead were not easy ones for Matthew. Matthew watched as Jonas at first simply fooled around with the dulcimer he had been given, awkwardly and carelessly striking at the strings. When Jonas was finally able to play a few tunes, he would often bring the beautifully crafted instrument to school where, at recess, he would play the tunes for others as they laughed and sang. Within a year or so, Jonas' dulcimer—though the tone was still good—had lost most of its luster, the wood marred with nicks and scratches, and some of the carving detail beginning to wear away. Matthew often found himself cringing at the way his friend handled the dulcimer.

The most difficult day came one spring afternoon when Matthew heard Jonas' father mention that Seth was coming over that night to ask Jonas if he would like to become the old man's apprentice and learn the craft of making dulcimers. The news stunned Matthew at first. He had never considered that Seth would want to take on an apprentice. Then, when the idea began to sink in, he felt crushed that the craftsman would have chosen Jonas over him. His love for the instruments ran deep, and he had always cared for them so well.

Matthew raced to Seth's cabin where he poured out his anguish to the old man, reminding him of the care he had given Seth's instruments and describing the condition of Jonas' dulcimer. Matthew continued by telling the craftsman how he cared for the dulcimer that was his—how he spent time each week polishing the wood, built a stand for it, and lovingly displayed it on a table at his house. He told how he played the instrument only on special occasions, always taking great care not to damage it, and how he avoided taking it away from the house lest it should be damaged.

The astonishment that first registered on Seth's face gradually softened to a gentle look of obvious compassion as he softly but firmly replied, "My son, I have not been unaware of your love for the dulcimers, nor have I been blind to Jonas' attitude toward them. Nevertheless, I believe Jonas has developed a greater and more appropriate appreciation for his gift.

"You see, I build the instruments not simply for the beauty of their appearance nor simply to make a living, but rather so that the music they produce can enrich the lives of others. I do take pride in my ability as a carver and finisher of wood, but that means very little if the instrument is not properly used. Jonas, because he understands this, will make a good craftsman.

"Matthew, my son, Jonas has shared his gift with others; you have carefully preserved yours. I can teach Jonas how to care for a dulcimer, but I cannot teach you how to share your gift; that is something you must develop on your own."

About Homer

When I first heard the ringing sound, I reached for the clock radio. The alarm was actually a buzzer, but at 2:35 A.M. logic takes time. After pressing all the buttons on the radio, my mind cleared enough to recognize that the sound was coming from the phone.

"Reverend Dukes?"

"Yes, Jessie," I replied. I knew the call was bringing bad news, and the realization helped me awaken. As a minister, such calls came with some degree of regularity, yet I never reached a point where I could take them into stride. Most of the time I knew where I would be going as soon as I answered the phone late at night—but that, too, was the nature of a small Georgia town. That night I would be going to Homer Jordan's house. Already the adrenaline was surging as I waited for Jessie to confirm my fear.

"Looks like tonight's the night. Horace wants you here," she said, her voice calm and soothing in spite of the circumstances. Jessie was a nurse with the hospice organization that served our county and two others. I was grateful for her call.

"Thanks Jessie, I'll get on over there."

Ellen, my wife, was propped on her left elbow. I turned on the small night light that illuminated the room just enough for me to dress. Although the light was dim, Ellen still blinked as she asked, "Is it Homer?"

"Yes. I'm afraid this is going to be it."

"Oh my," she sighed. Though still half asleep, the sincerity of her concern was evident in her voice. "Poor thing, he's had such a long struggle."

To some people, three years might not seem like such a long period of time, but three years of fighting a disease as relentless as lymphoma can seem like an eternity. Homer's fight had been a brave one, and I felt some sense of relief that it would soon be over.

As I drove out to Homer's farmhouse, I recalled the numerous times he had been in and out of hospitals over the past three years. At the last such visit one month before, Horace, his younger brother, told me there would be no point in hospitalizing him again. Homer knew he was going home to die, but said he preferred his "last small gasp of breath to be of fresh air." Homer never had been much for subtlety or beating around the bush.

Jessie entered the picture then. Her job was to make Homer as comfortable as possible, allowing him to die at home as he desired. She handled his medication, taught Horace to care for Homer, helped them obtain the equipment they needed, and helped both brothers come to terms with Homer's death. I was amazed at what she and the others in her organization were able to do.

As I turned into the dirt driveway, I could see the glimmer of the porch light. Homer's house was little more than a cottage next to Horace's house. Horace lived in the ancestral home, the one that was built by their grandfather.

Like many country homes, the structure was not fancy, but it was sturdy. The white, two-story dwelling had a porch that wrapped around three sides. What had once been a separate kitchen served as a garage.

Homer's house was next to Horace's, separated by a hedge. Homer built the four-room cottage himself, which was the primary reason he refused to leave it, even as his health rapidly deteriorated. The separate driveways, only a few feet apart, always amused me. Yet, a part of me understood and respected the arrangement.

Horace met me at the door. His face and the drooping of his shoulders made me realize how much of a struggle the last three years had been for him as well. I knew that, while Homer's struggle was coming to an end, Horace would yet have a ways to go.

"Thanks for coming, Preacher," Horace whispered—a whisper that gave a proper amount of reverence to the act of dying. As a child, I had equated dying with the game of hide-and-seek. Death was a hooded figure looking for the one weakened by illness or age. We whispered so as to avoid giving away the location of the weak one. I knew that the hushed tone signified resignation rather than hope.

As I took Horace's right hand in mine and placed my left hand on his shoulder, all I could say was, "I'm *so* sorry." This was one of those times when I wanted to say more and yet could not. When I began studying for the ministry, I was convinced that I would learn exactly what to say in such situations. But I learned that, unless you say something rude or incredibly insensitive, no one, in such a situation, will remember any of your words. They will remember you were there. They will also never forget if you were not there. But no one remembers your words. Experience had taught me that a sincere "I'm sorry" could say quite a lot. This was especially true of that night.

I was sorry for Homer's suffering—and for that of Horace. I was sorry for what I knew each would have to endure before the night was over, and I was sorry that I could not do more. I knew we could and would pray. I knew I would have to do some counseling with Horace. I knew I would have to speak to Homer, hoping that I could help him, in some way, deal with the relentless approach of "The Great Shadow." To be sure, I did not discount the value of such assistance and, yet, I invariably found myself wanting to do more. Perhaps the desire, to be more precise, was to do something more concrete, a desire that intensified when Horace spoke.

"He . . . he just looks so . . . so . . ." His voice trailed off as he lowered his head and breathed a great gulp of air. Throughout this ordeal I had not seen Horace's emotions break. I wondered when he would. He shuddered for a brief instant, and then I saw a single tear ooze across the brown hill that was his right cheek. I was relieved to see the tear, for I realized it could be the only sign of deep grief he would display.

Horace knew he did not need to finish the sentence. I patted his shoulder a couple of times and said, in a whisper of my own, "Let me step in there, Horace."

As I opened the door, my eyes quickly adjusted to the subdued light. Jessie was sitting on the bed, stethoscope in place, listening to Homer's heart or lungs. The pale thin body that was Homer seemed lost in the massive old bed. Homer's eyes were closed, the skin of his eyes and forehead shiny and smooth. His head was tilted back slightly, revealing the nostrils of his hooked nose. His mouth gaped open, dark and dry—the absence of his false teeth causing his cheeks to sink in and little wrinkles to form around his lips. The rest of his face that was visible above the blanket that covered him was shaded with a stubble of beard. Homer was no longer struggling to breathe as he had done the last few days.

Jessie had removed his oxygen, and the only sound was a faint rattle as he inhaled. Even I knew he would not be alive very long.

As I moved to stand beside Jessie, I could see the blood pressure cuff in place. Because of Homer's frail musculature, she had had to use a child's cuff. Jessie nodded and softly made her way to the door. I waited to see if Horace would enter the room, but he did not. I sat on the bed, taking Homer's already cold hand in mine. Still whispering, I said, "Homer, it's the preacher." No response. "Homer, I'm here with you, and I don't want you to be afraid. I know you've had a long struggle, but it's going to be over before long." His eyes fluttered, and he seemed to pull more air into his lungs.

"No, no," I said. "You rest and take it easy. I'm going to pray now. You just listen and relax."

I prayed for God's presence. I prayed for courage and strength, for faith and trust. I prayed that God would help us remember His promises to us. I prayed that God would give Homer peace and an absence of suffering. I could not have prayed for healing if I had wanted to do so. When the prayer was over, Jessie tip-toed back in. Her vigil had begun at five that afternoon. She had worked a full day and would be here for the duration. Homer was still, and the rattle resumed.

I left the bedroom and found Horace in the small kitchen. "How 'bout some coffee, Preacher?" he offered.

"Thanks, Horace," I said, taking and holding the mug while he poured.

"I sent Emma on to bed," he continued. "I kind of wanted to be here with just you and Jessie."

I was not surprised. Homer and Horace had been very close. Horace was all the family Homer had left, and Horace had done everything for Homer these last years. Though I was not surprised, I was touched. I felt honored that Horace wanted me there in this most intimate time.

We sat at the table to sip our coffee. Horace spoke while still staring into his cup of coffee, "I used to wonder how I would feel when this time came. You know—whether I'd be relieved or scared or sad or even happy. Now it's here, and I'm not sure I *can* feel. I'm just sort of numb."

"It's not unusual for people to feel numb at a time like this," I said. "Sometimes, going into shock is the only way the body can cope." I knew I had to be careful with my words. Even in his grief Horace was too sharp to let me get away with something trite or phony. "Horace, have you said your good-byes?"

"Yeah," he said with a sigh, "we talked some this morning. really there wasn't a lot to say. We're not the most talkative brothers, you know. But we've had time to say what needed to be said."

Even though he had stopped talking, as he glanced out the window over the sink he opened his mouth, clenched his left hand in a fist and then seemed to freeze momentarily before relaxing his hand and sighing again as he lowered his head. I was sure he wanted to say something else. I knew I could not push Horace, so I kept silent, letting him decide on his own if what he was thinking needed to be voiced.

After a few moments, he looked up with his eyes shining from tears. "Preacher, there was one thing I never told Homer—couldn't have told him. But it did bother me. In fact, I'm ashamed of it."

"What is it, Horace?" I asked, genuinely at a loss as to what he could mean.

He swallowed hard, took another sip of coffee and continued, "When . . . when Homer uh . . . got sick three years ago, I, uh . . . I didn't believe he had lymphoma."

Now I really was confused, "You didn't think he was sick?" I asked.

"No, no it wasn't that. It's just that for a while . . . I couldn't shake the thought that what he really had was . . . well . . . was AIDS."

Horace looked at me with eyes that were pleading—pleading for understanding, or absolution, or at least for an absence of condemnation. All I could manage to get out was, "Horace, why?"

"I don't know. His symptoms seemed to be consistent with what I was hearing. And, for a while there, he didn't talk about his illness much, even when I asked questions. Of course, I know Homer never said much to anybody his whole life. Anyway, I know what people must have thought about him. I know because, God forgive me, I wondered the same things."

"What things, Horace?"

"Well, that he was, well you know . . . funny."

"You mean you thought Homer was a homosexual?" I tried to make my voice sound gentle with no hint of accusation. I was taken by surprise. Seminary obviously did not prepare me for some things, and this was one of those things.

"Yeah, ho . . . homosexual, gay—whatever you're supposed to call it these days. Homer never married. He only had a few dates when we were young men. Never had that much interest in women. I guess I feel kind of guilty because I always helped Dad at the station. I mean, Homer ran the farm, but that also meant he was home with Mom most of the time. Then, when she got sick, he stayed here and cared for her."

"But, Horace, why should that make you feel guilty?"

"Well, maybe that forced him into it. Hell, I don't know, Preacher. Maybe, like I said, I really don't feel anything. I'm . . . well, I'm confused and I'm hurting; I can't make sense of anything right now."

I chose my words even more carefully than before, "Horace, Homer never gave any indication that he was gay. I really don't think you need to worry. Why, he was one of the most faithful church members and one of the best Sunday School teachers we've had. You know how much those third and fourth grade boys have missed him these last couple of years."

"Yeah, and I also know what some folks have said about him teaching that class over the years. They never said it right out in front of my face, but some would tell me what 'somebody else' had said. Plus some people would tell certain jokes or stories, knowing that I could hear, and then a couple of folks would cut their eyes toward me, and I had sense enough to know what that meant."

"But, Horace in all those years, all those years teaching those boys and taking the group fishing and coon hunting and camping, no one ever accused Homer of anything improper."

"I know, preacher, I know," he said with a sigh, "but you know when he would take those trips. You know, twice a year he'd be gone for two weeks. Well, he always left numbers where I could reach him. He always went to big cities, and most of the time it was San Francisco."

Had it been another person or another situation I would have challenged the assumption he was making, but not with Horace, not now. I did say, "And he told me on several occasions about museums he visited, about sites he visited in Washington and New York and Los Angeles and even in San Francisco."

"You're right, preacher, you're right but . . . I don't know. Something bothers me about that," he admitted.

"What bothers you Horace?" I had to push now. I had to get to the root cause of his anxiety as quickly as I could.

He sighed again, long and deep. He closed his eyes tightly, tilted his head back, breathed deeply, then exhaled as he brought his head back to an upright position. He looked me in the eye in a way that told me this was the heart of the matter, the seed from which this huge oak of anxiety and fear had sprung—having been watered and fertilized by the ignorance, fears, hatred, and prejudice of others. "Preacher, what if he is?" Horace asked as his lower lip began to tremble, and the fluid covered his eyes again. "What if he is gay? What happens, now—to his soul, I mean?"

The question was perfectly natural and logical. For a moment I wondered if Horace's concern was born out of selfishness; then I knew he was indeed focused on his brother. I decided to go for broke.

"Suppose he is gay, Horace," I said with my eyes focused on his. "Let's look at this a minute. He's a member of the church, so I assume he made a profession of faith in Christ."

"Yeah," Horace said, blinking at me as though he was emerging from sleep or a trance, "he did that when he was seventeen years old."

"O.K.," I said continuing, "now, he's been a faithful member of the church, attending regularly, giving regularly, helping out with projects. I know he's done a lot to minister to others. After your Mom died, as I understand it, he started giving one day a week to visit shut-ins, plus he taught that class of boys for twenty years, and no one ever complained of his actions with them. Why, even Jack Turner talked about Homer's influence when we ordained him to the ministry three years ago."

Horace had a far-away look in his eye. I guessed he was reminiscing. "They never elected him deacon, you know."

Now it was my turn to sigh, not at the recalcitrance of Horace but at the ignorance of my congregation, "Well, Horace, I kind of think it was their loss and their problem, because he acted more like a deacon than many that we have had."

Horace chuckled slightly at this, then stared at his now empty mug. After a moment his head bobbed slightly and quickly, then he looked up as if we were not quite finished. "But those trips, preacher, sometimes he got letters after them. Letters from people in those cities, but he never talked about it or them. I know, because we always got our mail at the station."

This was certainly not the time to challenge Horace for snooping into his brother's private life, so I simply said, "What of it, Horace?"

He responded rather strongly, "Come on preacher, don't you believe that gay stuff is wrong?"

Again I took great care in responding, "Horace I believe any sexual activity outside of marriage is wrong, just as I believe that any sin is wrong. But I do not believe that there are degrees of sinfulness. You and I do things that are wrong, too. I just believe that if God can forgive us, he can forgive Homer—whatever he may have done in his lifetime. I think Homer has as good a chance of going to be with God as you and I have."

At that point, Jessie stepped in the kitchen and said, "Horace, I doubt he'll last much longer." Her hand squeezed his shoulder; she was caring for two people.

Horace looked at me, his eyes wide with fear and apprehension, but I knew he did not fear death.

"Go ahead, Horace," I gently urged.

"I . . . I don't know that I can, Preacher. I'm well . . . I'm afraid or maybe embarrassed—maybe both."

"You don't have to be either, Horace," I said, more sure of myself. "He knows you loved him. You wouldn't have taken care of him all this time if you hadn't."

"But those . . ." Horace began, then after glancing at Jessie, "questions."

"I think Homer and God would both understand, Horace," I said as I rose and put my hand on his shoulder. "And besides, whether you believed them or not you still loved and treated him like the brother he was. I imagine that's all either one would ever ask of you."

Two days later, we buried Homer. That fall, at their suggestion, we renamed our young men's Bible study class, the "Homer Jordan Class." Horace gave them a framed portrait of Homer to hang in the room. No questions were asked.

The Burial

Randy had just removed the cover of the lawn mower's engine and had begun to check the fuel line. When he heard his dad call, he responded with "What?" as his eyes continued to follow the fuel line's course.

"Beth wants you on the phone," his dad said. Randy could hear the underlying tone of disapproval in Buck Wheeler's voice. Randy's mother had never interrupted Buck at work, and Buck thought those kinds of traditions ought to be protected and passed to each succeeding generation. Randy thought it was a crock for the most part.

Randy never dreamed that, at thirty-five years of age, he would be working with his dad at Wheeler's Farm and Garden Shop. Then again, who could have predicted the strange quirks of fate and personality that brought him here? The combination of a health conscious society and dwindling natural resources was supposed to have made marine biology a career of the future. The fact that the majority of the opportunities in the field of work lay outside the northwest corner of South Carolina was an even greater incentive. Two and one-half years of selling insurance to the "yacht set" in Miami simply allowed him to be relieved when the economic slump killed the career. By that time, Beth's mother had died, and her father's health had deteriorated. Although both Randy and Beth explored every possible option, they eventually were forced to move back home—more out of sensibility than economic necessity or desire.

Buck's life was fulfilled when Randy returned to work with him in the store. Now, five years later, Randy realized, even if Buck had not, that his dad needed him there. Sure, Buck could have hired someone to handle the physical aspects of the business, but Buck's mind was beginning to grow as feeble as his body. Randy knew Buck would never have let an outsider keep his books. If pushed, Randy would admit that being back home was not as awful as he and Beth had thought it would be.

Randy picked up the phone in the back and, still looking at and thinking about the mower, said, "Yeah?"

"Randy?" Beth said with a degree of hesitancy in her voice, "I wasn't sure if I should call, but Dr. Ford called to see when you would be home. I told him I wasn't sure and that he could call you at work, but he said he didn't want to bother you."

"Hmm," said Randy, finally turning from the mower, "you reckon I ought to give him a call?"

"Yeah, I think it might be a good idea," Beth replied.

"O.K., I'll let you know what I find out," Randy said, then he added, "Hey, could you look up the number for me?"

"Sure, hold on."

Dr. Ford was the retired pastor of their church. As long as Randy and Beth could remember, he had been at the church. They moved home five years ago, and a year later Dr. Ford's health forced him to retire. He was seventy-three, and arthritis and a bad heart had taken their toll, but his mind was still sharp. His wit and the sincerity and warmth that he exuded touched and won successive generations during his tenure at the church.

Beth gave Randy the number, and he depressed the phone cradle and dialed.

"Halloo . . ." Dr. Ford's lilting voice was one that fit him. There was comfort in its tone, a comfort that was soothing and inviting. Randy remembered that, even as a child, he had always felt drawn to this man. When Dr. Ford performed his and Beth's wedding ceremony, it was like having a beloved family member in charge of the service.

"Dr. Ford, this is Randy. Beth said you tried to call me a few minutes ago."

"Randy, how are you?"

"Oh, I'm fine. What can I do for you?"

"Oh nothing, nothing. I'm sorry Beth disturbed you."

"It's no bother at all. What's going on?"

Dr. Ford chuckled softly before saying, "Well, I declare. I just wondered if—by the way—don't you coach a youth basketball team at the church?"

"Yes sir, I do."

"Well, I wondered if you could suggest a young man I could hire to help me with something this afternoon."

"I'm sure I could. What do you need done?"

"Oh, just a little project."

Randy could tell that Dr. Ford was, in his own polite way, being evasive, and that piqued Randy's interest. "Is this something you need done today? Some of the guys may be tied up for a while after school."

"Yes, well, you see Evelyn's dog died this morning, and I wanted to get one of them to bury the dog in our back yard."

"Oh, I'm sorry," said Randy. He knew Mrs. Ford was devoted to her miniature daschund. The dog had been with them for years and was very protective, even barking and challenging those who came to visit the Fords. Randy paused for a moment, glancing out the small window at the steady drizzle that had been falling all morning. He knew it would be three to four hours before any of the boys could be reached. "Dr. Ford, I'll be right over," he said, hanging up before the older gentleman could protest. On his way out, he grabbed a shovel and a jacket.

"Where you goin'?" Buck asked.

"Got an errand to run, Dad. Be back in an hour or so." He could hear Buck mumbling as he went through the screened doors into the rain. He knew Buck thought Beth had called him home about something. Of course he also knew that if Beth had called Buck for something, Buck would have broken his neck getting to her side, even though he would have complained the whole way.

As Randy pulled around the drive behind the Ford's house, he could see Dr. Ford standing at the window. Before he reached the steps the older man had the door open and was saying, "I didn't want to take you away from your work. I can get someone to do this."

"I know you can, but I hate for you to have to wait. Where's Mrs. Ford?"

"She's lying down. This was difficult for her, although at his age we were not surprised. He just didn't wake up this morning."

Randy saw the dog lying in its bed in the kitchen. "Well, we need to get this done so that ya'll won't have to keep seeing him there. I know that must be tough."

"Hmm," said Dr. Ford, "I found a styrofoam ice chest in the storage room. We can put him in that. I believe she would like him buried near the bird bath in the azalea bed. But I wish you would just wait until I can get someone else. I don't want you to get muddy, and I know you've got work to do."

Randy just smiled and said, "Well, I hate to disappoint you, but I'm going to do this for you." He carefully placed the dog's body in the ice chest. The body had already stiffened; he hoped Dr. Ford had not seen him push to fit the body into the container. He placed the lid on top and positioned a rubber band that would hold it in place. He was relieved to see that Dr. Ford had been busy getting a jacket and umbrella out of a closet.

"No need for you to go out there," Randy said.

"No, no, I insist," replied Dr. Ford as he eased himself into his jacket. The task was slow and deliberate, for the arthritis had given the man a stooped back. He placed a hat on his head and reached for the aluminum cane he used for walking outside. "I'll hold the umbrella to keep the rain off you."

Randy was struck by the irony of the situation. He recalled when his mother and mother-in-law died. Each time Dr. Ford was there to comfort and minister to the families. Each time he unselfishly gave of his time and energy. He attended to their needs, even seeing that the church provided a meal on the day of the service in both cases. Now, when the shoe was on the other foot, the elderly minister could not let go and allow someone else to do something for him without feeling uncomfortable.

Then Randy thought: Perhaps this was something Dr. Ford needed to do—a kind of last gesture to a loving and faithful pet. People deal with death in different ways; maybe he needs to do this to get through this time. Mrs. Ford probably fell apart, and he feels he needs to be strong for her and for himself. He can't dig the hole, but, at least, he can assist the one who does. Randy was always amazed at the way older people became attached to pets they had for a long time, but he always thought, "I'll probably be that way, too."

Slowly they made their way to the azalea bed, shuffling though the wet autumn grass as the drumbeat of raindrops pelted the large black umbrella. The grass was thick and turning brown. Randy figured Dr. Ford was waiting for the last cutting of the season —no sense in paying someone to cut it when in another week or so it would not grow back.

"I hope the azalea bed won't be too muddy," said Dr. Ford.

"That's O.K. At least the ground will be soft," said Randy as they reached the border of the bed where the brownish grass gave way to the darker hues of wet pine straw.

Dr. Ford pointed with his cane to the spot where the grave was to be dug. Randy placed the chest to one side and stuck the blade of the shovel into the ground. The first few inches were mucky and yielded with a soft sucking noise, but beneath that layer the clay soil was a little more firm. Randy knew that, barring tree roots, this task would not take long.

"How long have you had this dog?" he asked, hoping the question would not make Dr. Ford uncomfortable.

"Oh, I think she got him eleven years ago. A friend gave him to her when he was still a pup." Dr. Ford reached out with his cane to pull back the wet pine straw. Soon he had cleared out an oval patch of wet mud just a bit larger than the ice chest. Randy began digging the outer edges. As he worked his way around, Dr. Ford followed him, dutifully holding the umbrella over Randy's head.

Randy focused on the ground, both to avoid slipping with the shovel and as an excuse to not stare at Dr. Ford. The gesture was one of respect—respect for the stature of the man and respect for his grief. He knew Dr. Ford to be a private man when it came to personal affairs. In his role as a minister, he was always open and accessible. People felt comfortable talking to him, and he was able to draw out of them their hopes and fears, dreams and nightmares, and passion and apathy.

Randy also remembered visiting Dr. Ford in the hospital after his heart surgery. The man waved off any inquiry about his condition, always saying "Oh I'm fine, just fine." In fact, most of the congregation was surprised when, less than a year after the surgery, he announced his decision to retire. No one suspected that his condition was that serious.

A strange feeling of warmth and satisfaction began to grow within Randy. At first he thought the rain had stopped and that, perhaps, the sun had begun to peek through the clouds, but as he glanced up he could see that the precipitation had not abated. The only sound other than raindrops was the soft scraping of the shovel entering the dirt and the plop of dirt added to the growing mound beside the hole.

When Randy judged that the hole was large enough and deep enough to accommodate the styrofoam coffin, he carefully lowered the container into the grave. Picking up the shovel again, he began to spade dirt and mud into the hole. Lost in thought and the strange feeling he was experiencing, he was a bit startled when he heard the clink of the shovel blade as it made contact with another piece of metal.

The blade of the shovel was lodged between the four-pronged base of Dr. Ford's aluminum cane. The stooped, white-haired man with his knotted fingers and drawn right hand was trying to push the dirt into the hole while continuing to hold the umbrella with his equally drawn and knotted left hand. Randy knelt to dislodge the shovel.

As he stood, he looked into Dr. Ford's eyes for the first time. In those eyes he saw surprise, perhaps a bit of fear, and discomfort at the least. Quickly, Dr. Ford looked away as, again, he began to poke at the mound of dirt. With his own left hand, Randy gently stilled the hand that held the cane, and with his right hand, Randy took the umbrella. They stood that way for a moment until Dr. Ford slowly glanced again at Randy's face. There was uncertainty in the old man's faded blue eyes, a sense of lostness.

In a hoarse whisper Randy said, "It's O.K. Really it's O.K." The eyes softened, and Randy thought he heard a brief sigh.

The feeling of awkwardness that overwhelmed Randy came with sudden and unrelenting force. He folded the umbrella and stuck its point in the ground. Feeling himself at a loss for words, he quickly grabbed the shovel and finished filling in the hole. He left the low mound uncovered, and he stood, eyes cast down, not knowing what to do or say.

Dr. Ford pulled the umbrella out of the ground and—extending his right hand—said, "Thank you, Randy. I do appreciate this."

"I'm . . . . I'm sorry," Randy said as he lightly shook the hand that looked more frail than before. "I know how much this dog must have meant to you," he said, still not able to look Dr. Ford in the eye.

After the briefest pause, Dr. Ford said, "Meant a lot to Evelyn. Actually, I never could stand the damn thing."

Randy's eyes snapped up to meet Dr. Ford's. Several seconds elapsed before he could accept that he had indeed heard those words from the lips of the old minister.

Finally both men broke into laughter. They turned and started back to the house, Dr. Ford carrying the cane and Randy carrying the shovel and the umbrella. After a few steps, Dr. Ford reached out and up to place a reassuring arm around Randy's shoulders.

The gesture brought back countless memories for Randy but, to his knowledge, it was the first time he had responded by placing an arm around the minister's shoulders. Together, like that, they made their way through the drizzle to the warmth and comfort of the house.

The
Elements
of
Surprise

I think we all have a tendency to get used to a certain system or way of doing things and are thereby lulled into a false sense of security. We honestly believe that the system is fool-proof and, thus, give it little or no thought. Then, on the one inevitable occasion when the system fails, we are particularly unprepared to deal with the consequences. I also believe that no other institution in the universe is more prone to this scenario than the church. Church ritual is usually based more on what our grandparents and great-grandparents did and thought than on any portion of scripture.

Sandy Run Baptist Church, close by the Georgia bank of the Savannah River, was a very comfortable rural church, in part because it held fast to the unwritten law of "system maintenance." The congregation of Sandy Run was sizable for a rural church. It represented a limited diversity of occupations and a somewhat less diversity of socio-economic status. Basically, one's livelihood came from agriculture or the "Bumb Plant"—to use the local vernacular.

The "Bumb Plant" was the Savannah River Nuclear Facility, a place that produced the plutonium used in nuclear warheads. There was always an air of secrecy about those who worked at the Savannah River Plant, or SRP as it was designated by the newspapers. Parents often cautioned their children not to ask the specific duties of persons who worked at SRP. Apparently such information, if it leaked, could pose a threat to our national security. I suppose it made sense to a child.

It was a different matter when, as an adult, a person somehow learned that some of these people were gate guards who rarely ventured more than five feet past the gate houses that were situated on the distant perimeters of the vast property that contained SRP. Other workers were janitors, or maids, or fork-lift operators. We did have a couple of management people in our congregation, but I never encountered anyone who had hands-on responsibility for producing the business end of a nuclear bomb.

A few shopkeepers were in our congregation, along with a group of retirees and one or two folks who worked in Augusta, but the majority of our congregation was tied to the land. We had loggers who worked for the Continental Can paper company. Four families owned large tracts of land on which they grew timber and planted corn, soybeans, and cotton. Two of those families also maintained peach and pecan orchards. The other people in our church worked for these families or leased smaller farm tracts from them.

All in all, this congregation was rather tradition-bound, though loving. I became its pastor three years prior. My wife and I bought a small tract of land with a pond and small peach orchard. At age sixty I was tired of the city rat-race and planned to finish my ministry there, becoming a full-time retiree at age sixty-five. I suppose, in many ways, the church and I were quite a good fit. After thirty-five years of developing and pushing innovative programs, I was more than ready to shift into the "maintenance mode" with which this congregation seemed so comfortable.

The mutual sense of comfort caused us to be very unprepared for our first Sunday in April. We were scheduled to observe the Lord's Supper, which was observed with strict regularity on the first Sunday of each quarter. I had adjusted to saying "the Lord's Supper" rather than "communion," the term we used in most of the other churches I served.

I was in my office at 9:30 going over notes for my sermon that would focus on the fellowship aspects of the ordinance. My study was interrupted by the sudden appearance of Mrs. Inez Lyons. This appearance was not a vision; she barged through the door of my office, a habit of hers that I found extremely irritating. Choking back my irritation as well as my pride, I forced a smile and asked, "What is it, Inez?"

"It's gone," she gasped.

I resisted the temptation to ask if she was referring to her girdle. (Mrs. Lyons was a rather sturdy individual.) She could also be somewhat intimidating to those who did not know her well. For years Mrs. Lyons and her husband, Frank, both employees of SRP, had taken responsibility for preparing the elements for communion. Saturday afternoon they were at the church washing and shining each serving piece. On the day of communion, they spent the Sunday School hour breaking the saltine crackers into pieces on the flat trays and filling the small glasses with Welch's grape juice.

Like I said, church ritual grows out of our ancestors' opinion instead of scripture. Scripture says that Christ used wine and unleavened bread, but our forebears considered drinking a sin (or, at least, that was their public position on the matter), and a loaf of bread that did not rise a disgrace. So we were left with saltines and room-temperature Welch's juice—poor second cousins to the original elements.

It so happened that Inez was referring to those poor second cousins. Her hand went to the base of her throat as she rasped, "The bread . . . the, the juice . . . it's all gone."

Obviously I had not grasped the gravity of the situation. I simply shrugged and said I was sure there was enough in the kitchen pantry.

"No, no," she said, her eyes changing from the white-dominated stare of shock to the blazing red of anger. "We had just enough for today, and I had it in the closet with the serving pieces, and now it's all gone!"

I was weighing the options before us—which did not suit Mrs. Lyons at all. She was a woman of action and expected me to follow her lead. "Get up," she practically screamed "come look at this!"

The closet was behind the front part of the sanctuary. Actually, it was more like a small kitchen with a sink and storage facilities. The cupboard above the sink was indeed bare.

"Did you look in the other cupboards?" I asked, with immediate regret. I knew Mrs. Lyons would be insulted, but the situation was still kind of strange, and I did not see any need for panic—but then I had not been preparing the elements for twenty-three years as Mrs. Lyons and her husband had.

"Yes, I looked everywhere," Mrs. Lyons said. "I'll bet it was one of those Turner boys. Probably came here first thing. I'm telling you pastor, locking the cabinet where we keep the serving pieces just isn't enough; we need to put a lock on this door too."

"Now, now Mrs. Lyons," I said, trying to calm her down, "I know you got here before 9:30 this morning and no one else was here then except me, and I ate breakfast at home today"—a vain effort at trying to lighten the mood with a little humor.

Obviously, Mrs. Lyons was in no mood for humor. All I received in return was an icy stare and awkward silence. Fortunately, Mr. Lyons appeared at this time. Frank Lyons was a small, thin man with a bright pink complexion. Close-cut, white hair wrapped around his head from ear to ear, stopping just a couple of inches above his ears. When he was worried or nervous, as he almost always seemed to be, wrinkles formed pink waves across his forehead and continued through the bald spot on top. I figured Mr. and Mrs. Lyons to be a perfect match. She was a strong, opinionated, domineering woman, and he seemed content to let her be just that.

"Oh preacher, this is just awful," he said, "but I found something ya'll ought to see." He whirled around and headed toward the sanctuary. Mrs. Lyons pushed past me to follow him, with me being swept along in her wake.

When I reached the sanctuary, they were standing at the second pew from the front, looking at the floor. There, beneath the front pew, was an empty saltine box and two empty quart bottles of Welch's grape juice. We all stood there a moment as we pondered the mystery. In fact we were so engrossed with our speculations that Frank and I, but not Mrs. Lyons, jumped when a voice behind us said, "Hey thar."

We turned to see Cooter Barnes standing with a wide grin on his face. Cooter was usually described by people in the community as "not being quite right." Really, Cooter was just child-like. He lived in a small house on one of the larger farms, one for which his parents had worked. Apparently, he got a government check each month and did odd chores here and there to make a living. I guess he did not need a great deal of money. He raised vegetables in a small garden behind his house and was always hunting and fishing. Folks in the community knew him and looked out for him.

Cooter saw the bottles and box on the floor and asked, "Somebody have a picnic?"

Mrs. Lyons looked at him with a wild-eyed expression. Fearing what she might say, I beat her to the punch and said, "Well, someone has eaten the crackers and juice we use for the Lord's Supper."

"Musta' been kinda' a trashy person to leave that stuff on the flo' like that," Cooter said, "plus they done got mud on the pew cushion." (I had not even noticed.) Cooter pushed through us into the pew, peering at the floor beyond the bottles and box. "They's some tracks here goin' off yonder," he said. We followed what were, to me at least, barely perceptible traces of red mud on the carpet. The trail led to the old choir room behind the sanctuary—a room that was now used, primarily, for storage. "Looka' yonder," Cooter said.

A window had been broken in the room. "Musta' been somebody passin' through. Bet they come in here ta' sleep on the pews and got hongry 'n' found them crackers an' juice."

"Oh, good Lord," said Mrs. Lyons with a look of disgust on her face. Mr. Lyons just stood there shaking his head, the pink waves on top shimmering in the light and revealing the sheen of perspiration he had developed. He removed a white handkerchief from his pocket and wiped his forehead as he mumbled under his breath and shook his head once again.

"Well," I said, "I don't see why we can't just postpone the Lord's Supper until next week." I knew I had made a mistake when I heard Mrs. Lyons' sharp intake of breath, followed by a sputtering sound as she fought for the words that would best express her feelings.

Finally she came out with, "Well I never . . .," followed by, "Pastor we haven't missed a Lord's Supper in twenty-three years nor in the forty-seven before that when Mr. and Mrs. Grayson prepared the elements. They told us that when we took over for them. I'm not going to let it happen now."

I noticed a panicky look on Mr. Lyons' face. I knew I had to think quick. His hands were starting to shake as the perspiration began to cascade down his forehead. I felt my own hands clenching with tension. Then, I had an idea: "The Minit Mart over at the crossroads should be open," I said as I reached for my wallet. "We can probably get what we need there."

Cooter jumped in quickly, "Yeah, that's an idea. I'd be glad ta' go." Cooter always wanted to be of help. The only problem was that people rarely trusted him or believed he could be of help. Mrs. Lyons was such a person.

"No, no, we can't do that," she said. "Frank can go. Go on Frank," she snapped.

Frank jumped and looked at me with an expression of confusion and helplessness. Again, I noted the trembling of his hands. I wondered just what his job was at the "Bumb Plant," but it was only a fleeting thought. No way would I let him get on the road in his condition!

This situation should not have been such a problem. In fact, communion was not the problem at all; the problem was Mrs. Lyons' reputation, and I sensed that should it suffer, we would all suffer. "Tell you what," I said, "I'd really like for Frank to help clean up that mess in the sanctuary. We certainly can't have anyone sitting in that mud on the pew. Cooter you need to get us a big box of saltines or two small ones and two quarts of Welch's grape juice. Now, have you got that?" I asked as I placed a twenty dollar bill in his hand. I did not even bother with reminding him about bringing back the change. It could just be an investment in my sanity.

"Gotcha' preacher," Cooter said, and he was on his way. I had out-flanked Mrs. Lyons. I noted with gratitude that she hurried Mr. Lyons to the supply closet for the cleaning supplies they needed to take care of the pew. I was foolish enough to think that the crisis had been weathered when, in reality, we were merely experiencing the deceptive calm of the passing of the hurricane's eye.

I retrieved my notes from the office and was opening the large pulpit Bible to the scripture text of the day when I saw Cooter enter with a brown grocery bag. He just smiled and waved as he rushed behind the chancel. I had just completed arranging things on the pulpit when I heard the sounds. There was an almost breathless "Oh, my Lord!" followed by a loud "thud" that echoed through the sanctuary.

Rushing to the small kitchen, I found Cooter standing there with a confused expression. Mr. Lyons was kneeling on the floor, shaking his head and mumbling as though seized by a charismatic episode, while tidal waves of glistening pink flesh rolled across the top of his head. His handkerchief was clutched in his right hand as he frantically waved it back and forth in front of his wife's face. Mrs. Lyons was on the floor; her head was in his lap, eyes closed and mouth sagging open. She had fainted.

"What happened?" I asked.

Mr. Lyons continued his incoherent mumbling but, with his right hand, he did manage to point to the counter. There on the counter was the empty bag, and beside it was a pair of two-liter R.C. colas and a box of Moonpies.

I turned back into the hallway and pressed the back of my hand to my mouth. I knew I could not laugh the way I wanted to laugh. Hearing movement behind me, I turned to see Mrs. Lyons struggling to her feet. "Look at this," she said as tears began to well in her eyes. "Look, look, loo . . .," her voice trailed off as she slumped back onto her husband—who was almost crushed between her and the door-jamb.

"Cooter, what happened?" I asked, fighting for composure. There was only a faint flutter in my voice to indicate my struggle to suppress the laughter.

"Nothin' happen't, preacher," Cooter said, smiling again. "They wuz outta' sody crackers, an' Louise said they ain't never carried no Welch's. They did have summa' that 'Jolly Aid' grape drink mix—but that stuff's awful, plus I figgered we wouldn't have time to get sugar an' mix it up. I did give a thought to them grape 'Nehis,' but all they had wuz twelve ounce bottles 'n' cans—so's I just got these R.C.'s. The Moonpies wuz right nex' ta them drinks."

Mrs. Lyons was now trying to compose herself, although I guessed she was struggling with anger. "Cooter," she said slowly and with a great deal of effort, "we can't use cola and Moonpies for the Lord's Supper."

"We cain't?" Cooter replied with genuine astonishment.

"No, it would be a sacrilege," she gasped, her tone a bit sharper now.

"A sack-a-what?" Cooter asked, still without a clue.

"Cooter," I interjected, "some people might think we were mocking—uh, 'making fun' of the Lord's Supper if we use this."

"Really?" Cooter asked as he looked back at the counter and scratched his head.

"Yes, you foo . . ." My quick stare cut short Mrs. Lyon's response.

"Well, mebbe' so," Cooter drawled, "but don't the Bible say Jesus and his men used wine and bread?"

"Yes, that's right," I said.

"Well I don't see whar whut we got here is that much further off than Welch's and sody crackers."

"Hmmpf!" said Mrs. Lyons, and then, "You see Cooter, Jesus used wine and unleavened or flat bread because that was a natural part of the Passover meal. The grape juice comes from the same fruit as the wine, but it's not intoxicating, and the saltines are flat pieces of bread."

"So he jest used part of their regular meal, right?" asked Cooter.

"Right," Mrs. Lyons and I said.

Again Cooter broke into grin, "Well then, we's O.K. Me and half the folks in this church drink R.C.'s 'n' eat Moonpies for lunch probably two or three times a week. Shoot, Mr. Lyons, don't you?"

Mr. Lyons piped up with, "Well, yeah, that does sort of make sense . . ." His voice trailed off as he caught the look on Mrs. Lyons' face.

I happened to glance at my watch and realized it was 10:30. "Look," I said, "if we are going to have the Lord's Supper this morning, I don't think we have any choice."

Mrs. Lyons sighed, "Perhaps we don't, but I still don't like it."

"I know you don't," I said, "but I'll try to make it work." How—I did not know.

"Come on Frank," she said "we had better get busy." Then, shaking her head as she opened a Moonpie, she continued, "But they're just so common." That phrase gave birth to inspiration.

In the morning meditation I related how the juice and crackers had been taken. I reminded our folks that if a person was that hungry, God would probably have preferred that our crackers and juice be used to satisfy the hunger. I told them of the dedication to their task displayed by the Lyons and of Cooter's willingness to be of help and how he had brought back the only things he could find: R.C. colas and Moonpies.

I believe, at first, most persons in the congregation thought I was building up to a joke. They were waiting for the punch-line, but then I told them that the Lyons,' Cooter, and I realized R.C. colas and Moonpies were sort of common—just as wine and unleavened bread were common elements of the Passover meal.

I suggested that Jesus selected them for this reason and that he was telling the disciples and us that the gospel would be communicated through common folks—ordinary people like Luke and Matthew; Peter and John; the Lyons, Cooter, me, and the rest of the people gathered there that day—and common means such as ordinary conversation, fellowship, and the sharing of a meal. I told them we were mistaken to think that only special people can be chosen and used by God or that worship can take place only at special times and in special buildings. Further, I said it was time we recovered the "wonderful ordinariness" of the gospel.

I believe I noticed some changes in our folks after that day. They had a different spirit. More of them were willing to teach, pray, and lead. We never again used saltines and grape juice for the Lord's Supper, but we did not use R.C. cola and Moonpies either. Instead our deacons voted that we would use rolled-out flat biscuits and sweet tea and that folks in the church would take turns making the elements. Mr. and Mrs. Lyons continued preparing the elements, and we continued to call our observance the Lord's Supper. From that point on, however, the spirit of fellowship in communion observances was richer and sweeter than any Moonpie I have ever tasted.

The Sign

I suppose any job has certain tasks that are unappealing, to say the least. In some jobs a person is expected to hate the work, almost as if despising the work is a prerequisite. I certainly cannot imagine the Roto-rooter man beaming with pride as he proclaims, "Man, I love the smell of sewage in the morning!" I do not think I could trust a Roto-rooter man who loves his work. A minister does not have just a job, but a calling, which apparently means he or she is supposed to love every task—even those aspects of the work for which the person is ill-suited.

One of my least favorite tasks as a minister was visiting a friend or distant relative of one of my church members when the friend or relative had apparently gone "off their rocker" (a theological/pastoral term derived from Christ's nickname for the apostle Peter [Rock] who, on occasion, demonstrated some rather bizarre behavior of his own). Usually one of the older ladies, as she left church after the Sunday morning service, would squeeze my hand particularly tight. With a furtive glance to either side she would say, "Pastor, there's someone you need to see"—at which point I would inwardly cringe.

I was always struck by the choice of words: someone I "need to see." Half of the time I wanted to say, "The only people I 'need' to see are the ones who are starting for the Atlanta Braves this afternoon." I think that watching baseball fascinated me because, for a couple of hours, I could watch nine grown men do what needed to be done without me having to tell them to do it. Even more impressive, nine times out of ten, these guys worked together to achieve their objective. The world of baseball was so far removed from the world of the church. In baseball they yelled, "I've got it!" rather than, "You're gonna' get it!"

At any rate, as soon as I heard a person say "someone you need to see," I knew the words would become a self-fulfilling prophecy—primarily because I knew this member of my church would mention the friend or relative every time she saw me until I made the visit. I could baptize 500 new members, raise a million dollars in a month, write ten books, and visit each member of the congregation every week. Yet, this one church member would say,

"What do you suppose he does with his time?" unless I visited the friend or relative.

I found myself sweating away in the over-heated interior of my beige Chevy Caprice on one Sunday afternoon as I headed for the edge of town to see Mrs. Mamie Suttle, who lived in a mobile home just off the main highway. I had never met her before and, in fact, did not know she existed until that morning when Mrs. Ruby Henry told me about Mrs. Suttle, her second cousin on her father's side. Actually, I had heard about Mrs. Suttle, though I did not know who she was.

For a few weeks, word had been going around town that a woman had seen the face of Christ in the living room ceiling of her mobile home. At first I thought people were repeating a headline they had seen in the *National Enquirer*. Soon, however, I learned that this story was a local phenomenon. Perhaps the name had not stuck with me because most people were overcome with giggles and snickering when they told the story. Apparently, the situation had become an embarrassment for Mrs. Henry. She was a rather somber and staid member of the community—a Sunday School teacher, chairwoman of the church flower committee, and a founding pillar of the W.M.U.

Mrs. Henry informed me that her cousin Mamie had "just never been right" since her husband, Osborne, died. Upon inquiring, I learned that Mr. Suttle had been dead for thirty-one years, which made me wonder if I was about to discover a world record for grief avoidance. This was the only information Mrs. Henry would give me, other than to mention that she had told Mrs. Suttle I would drop by the first chance I got.

In essence, Ruby had diagnosed her cousin's problem, and she was anxious for me to drop by and confirm her diagnosis with my second opinion. I, of course, was much cheaper, much less embarrassing, and much more amenable than a psychiatrist. Amenable I was, for, after all, it is bad enough to get fired from a job, but how does one face being fired from a calling?—"I'm sorry, but we have determined that, contrary to your misguided beliefs, God was not leading you into the ministry."

When I reached Mamie Suttle's drive, I realized I had seen her trailer before. The structure itself was unremarkable, but the front yard contained a cement bird bath with faded purple plastic flowers "planted" around it. I had always noticed the bird bath and flowers when I had driven by. The yard consisted of patchy grass and weeds, not an immaculate yard but neat nevertheless. On either side of her front steps were spindly rose bushes, one red and one yellow, with each shrub sporting two full blooms and the red one including a small bud.

I went to the house and knocked on the loose screen door, causing it to bang against the doorjamb and make more noise than I intended. From inside I heard a shrill, high-pitched voice call out, "Just a minute."

Soon the door opened to reveal a short woman with a round face and graying, brown hair pulled back in a bun. She wore glasses with thin, gold, wire frames. Her dress looked out of date, though I could imagine that in its time it must have been quite nice. Her skin was smooth and white, and her face bore a pleasant smile—though her eyes seemed to wander about as though she was not sure she was seeing everything she should see.

Before I could introduce myself, the woman opened the screen door and said, "Come right on in. You're the first visitor today; most don't arrive until 2:30 or 3:00."

I interrupted her to tell her who I was, all the while thinking that she had just opened her door to a complete stranger. I had begun to think that Ruby was right: This lady was a danger to herself and certainly needed help. I watched as she hobbled closer to me, as if to finally get a good look at me.

"So you're Reverend Timms. Ruby just thinks you're wonderful. Says she's never heard a better preacher. I hear you sometimes on the radio, if I don't watch preaching on the T.V."

By this time she had taken my hand, and we were making our way to her couch that was covered with a gold corduroy bedspread. Beige curtains with a gold, tasseled trim hung from the windows. We negotiated around a scarred wooden coffee table on top of which was a large print *Reader's Digest*, a large print King James Bible, a Sunday School book, a devotional book, a magnifying glass, and a jar of peppermint candy. As we sat, I noticed the room also contained a small television and an upholstered rocking chair. Beside the chair was a small table with magazines and a couple of books. Behind the chair was a floor lamp with a black metal shade. The lamp reached almost to the ceiling in that corner of the room. The room opened to a dining area that contained a small antique china cabinet and a metal, formica-topped table with three metal chairs.

Mrs. Suttle seemed to sit in slow motion, finally collapsing on the couch with a sigh. After rearranging her dress, she turned to me and said in an apologetic tone, "I hate to be so feeble, but this arthritis slows me up a bit."

I told her that was alright and then asked her how she had been doing. She responded that—other than the pain in her knees, her racing heartbeat, and shortness of breath—she was feeling pretty good. She said that getting up and down to let visitors in aggravated the pain in her knees. She estimated that five or six people came by on weekday afternoons and evenings and some-times a dozen or more on Saturday and Sunday.

One thing I could say for her, she did not put on a front for anyone. While the trailer was not what I would call dirty, it cer-tainly was not immaculate. I asked if she ever hesitated to let any of these strangers come into her house. The question produced a blank stare. I wondered for a moment if I had let a word of pro-fanity slip.

Finally, Mrs. Suttle spoke, saying, "Why, no, preacher, I never worry about those who come. After all, if God has given me this sign and it can help people, I have to share it with them. After all, if you can't trust the Lord, who can you trust?"

I wanted to take issue with her beliefs about God's protection, but I realized I would never get anywhere—at least not now. In-stead, I asked what she had meant when she said her "sign" helped people.

"Oh," she began as her face brightened, "a lot of people pray when they see the sign. Some are in pain or feel real bad, and almost all of them are healed before they leave. Some have come back to tell me they were out of work when they visited, but got a job the next week. Several marriages have been saved."

"And the only explanation for all of this is this sign?" I asked.

"Well, preacher," she said, "between you and me, I've known a few of those people for years, and some who claimed they were healed never had much of a problem to begin with."

Her candor and apparent lucidity caught me off-guard, and the only response I could manage was, "Ma'am?"

"I think the problem with some of these people is all in their heads. And most of them just don't trust doctors, particularly doctors who say there's nothing physically wrong with them. Of course, who knows, some of them may just need to believe in something, and maybe they get so excited when they see the sign that they—for a little while, at least—forget about what's supposed to be ailing them."

I marveled at the presumptuous manner in which I had considered instructing this woman on the fine points of theology and psychology. I did feel safe enough to prod her just a bit with what I considered to be an appropriate question, however. "Has the sign 'helped' you in any way? I mean you still have your arthritis . . ." My voice trailed off as I began to fear that I had pushed too far.

She paused for a moment as a strange look came over her face, a look brought by pleasant memories almost shrouded by time and more recent memories that were not so pleasant. At first, I mistook this look for a sign of confusion, but when she spoke, she spoke with amazing clarity.

"Well, yes, I suppose I do 'still have my arthritis,' as you put it. But let me tell you something. For a long time now I have been alone. My husband died over thirty years ago, and the Lord never saw fit to give us children. In addition to being alone, I've had my share of disappointment in life.

"Besides my husband's untimely death and the absence of children, I've lost most of what Mr. Suttle and I managed to accumulate before his death. I'm sure you've seen the large white house at the end of Oak Street. That was Mr. Suttle's family home. I stayed there for ten years after his death, but then had to sell it because I couldn't have kept paying the taxes and would not have been able to keep it up. That alienated most of my husband's family, distant though they had been. Perhaps, as they thought, I should have been able to get a job, but I had prepared for life as a wife and mother.

"Though I was then neither, I could not find the energy, courage, or whatever to seek a position. I simplified my life. Now, most people think me to be strange, or crazy, or mean, or selfish. Few have visited me over the years; hardly any could be called friends.

"Now, you see, I have the sign, and people come to see the sign. They visit with me, and while they are visiting, I am able to do something I could not do for the last fifteen years or so: I can stop thinking about the pain of my arthritis. So, no, God has not 'taken it away,' but He has given me relief. That may be crazy, but, if so, I am content in my madness."

There was nothing left to say, particularly from me. Her brief, simple story awed me with its insight, candor, pain, and triumph. Finally, I managed to mumble, "May I see?"

Slowly, Mrs. Suttle rose and hobbled over to the black-shaded floor lamp and with a deliberate and slow gesture turned the switch. The corner of the ceiling was bathed in an amber light that curved in an exact line on one end and spread to dimness on the other. To be honest, I am not sure I saw anything. Some bumps in the blown-ceiling panel formed a narrow oval, and I suppose some people would make a face out of what was there, but I saw nothing other than the random grouping of bumps.

Of course, I did not need the sign. I had already received "a blessing" in my encounter with this elderly woman. Who was I to say how God would answer the prayers and needs of this woman and those who came to see the "sign" God had given to her? Perhaps my blindness to the sign was due to the frail nature of my own faith. Perhaps madness is the province of those of us who are so quick in our judgments, so selective in our acceptance, and so arrogant in our belief.

I left prepared to tell Mrs. Ruby Henry that perhaps we were the ones who were crazy, for Mrs. Mamie Suttle seemed fine to me. Such a statement would be risky, and I knew it could cause me some real problems. But what if it did? Maybe then I, too, would be able to see the sign.

The Penny War

If I had been older than age twelve, perhaps I would have been dreaming about girls, but almost all of my dreams at the time were about baseball. I was a short-stop and pitcher for a good team, and I was constantly dreaming about winning the Little League championship. This time I had just hit a line drive toward the chainlink fence in left field. I wanted the ball to go over and yelled, "Get up! Get up!"

"Get up, Son." The voice was that of my dad awakening me. The clock read 6:45, and we needed to open the gas station at 7:00 A.M. Rolling out of bed, I pulled on my jeans and tee-shirt and began lacing up my tennis shoes. At Christmas, the high-top Converse shoes had been stiff and black. Now, in July, the canvas was soft, and the color was that of the ashes in a charcoal fire.

Mom had left a ham biscuit on the table for me. I grabbed it as I headed out the door. Dad was waiting in the truck. His body dwarfed the steering wheel and seemed cramped in the cab of the Ford pickup. He was six-feet-four and weighed 265 pounds. His name was Dewey, like mine, but for him the name did not seem to fit. The folks in town just called him "Big 'Un."

Dad shifted into reverse as I climbed in. Turning to look over his shoulder, he draped his massive right arm over the top of the seat and tousled my hair as he asked, "That arm feel O.K.?"

"Yes sir," I replied, "it's fine."

"Well, you pitched a good game last night."

"Thanks," I said, grinning so much that biscuit crumbs fell out of my mouth and onto my lap and the black vinyl of the seat.

As he shifted into first gear, Dad continued, "And I'm proud of you for not ragging that Turner kid."

Tommy Turner was a nice enough guy, but not a ball-player. The night before, he hit a weak grounder to third base. Trying to run to first, he tripped over his own feet and sprawled in the red dust. Everyone laughed and for the rest of the night teased him unmercifully. Dad was right: I did not join the others, although I am not sure why; just as, now, I was not sure what to say in response to my father's praise.

We rode in silence until we pulled up behind the station. The rising sun gave an orange tint to the blue and white Pure Oil sign on the corner. The dampness that caused my shirt to stick to the vinyl seat, even at this early hour, let me know that the day would be a scorcher. Dad used to say that the heat and humidity of a Georgia July day could make fire sweat.

As soon as the door was unlocked, I grabbed a mop, bucket, and rag and headed for the bathrooms around back. Dad insisted that they be as clean as ours at home. My mom made that a challenge. When I finished and came back in the office, Dad was putting money into the cash register as he took a swallow from a Coca-Cola bottle.

The drinks were kept in a metal box full of chipped ice. He had just replaced the ice for the day, a chore I would repeat at closing. I never tasted a colder liquid than the drinks that came out of the ice. Several times a day, groups of three or four men would gather around the box, and each would pull out a six-ounce Coca-Cola. Then, turning the bottles over, they would call out the name of the town on the bottom of the bottle. The person whose bottle originated in the town closest to ours paid for everyone's drink. They called it Coke-poker, and it was the only kind of gambling my Dad allowed at his business.

Looking at some papers the gas company had sent him, Dad called me over: "Son, go out there and change the price on the sign to twenty-six and nine; I'll take care of the pumps." Gas had gone up a penny. On the way out, I noticed that Wilbur was craning his neck to see the numbers I held.

Wilbur operated the station and mini-grocery across the street. He called it Wilbur's One-Stop. Wilbur carried a few food items and a lot more candy and gum than my Dad and always kept his gas price one penny under my Dad's price. If Dad went up, Wilbur went up. If Dad's price went down, Wilbur went down. As soon as the new numbers were in place, I saw Wilbur go to his storage room. A few minutes later he came out with his new price.

Wilbur was a short, balding, thin man with a smooth complexion and a face that was bright red—even in the midst of winter.

His grayish-blue eyes always seemed to be bulging out of their sockets. Wilbur seemed to hurry wherever he went. He walked fast, slamming his feet onto the hot concrete. Wilbur fumbled with the metal panels on his A-frame sign until he had posted his new price of twenty-five and nine; and then, on his way inside, he stopped and changed his pumps.

Dad and I were standing in the doorway of our station as Wilbur changed his price. As Wilbur headed back inside, Dad shook his head and chuckled, "That Wilbur is a piece-a-work, ain't he?" I just laughed and nodded as I headed back to stand in front of the big, black, pedestal fan.

The fan was positioned behind the drink box so that the cool air from the ice water was distributed in the office area. Wilbur had two window unit air-conditioners for his little store. I had been in there before and knew those two units could not cool his place as well as our fan and drink-box cooled our office. In fact, this was one of the main reasons my Dad had resisted the idea of replacing the drink box with a machine. He kept saying that as long as he could get ice, he would keep the box. We were lucky that an ice-house a block behind us managed to stay open. Dad said there were not many places like it left. Our store stayed open by storing meat for people.

"Dong! Ding!" The first customer of the day pulled up. Roy Tiner was climbing out of his truck as I got to the pumps. "Hey, Mr. Tiner," I said. "Fill'er up?"

"Hey there, Dewey," he said. Then, after spitting a brown stream of tobacco juice, he continued, "Yep, give 'er all she'll take." He headed toward the office calling out, "Hey, Big 'Un, I hope them Coky-Colers is cold."

As I pumped Mr. Tiner's gas, I noticed Wilbur was fiddling with his air conditioners. As I watched, Buford Weems pulled up in his shiny black Oldsmobile. Mr. Weems was a lawyer and bought a brand new Olds every other year. Each one was black with black interior. Mr. Weems picked up a loaf of bread and headed over to Wilbur.

I knew Wilbur was mad. Mr. Weems always bought bread and other food items from him, but he bought his gas from us. Sure enough, Mr. Weems pulled out of Wilbur's lot and right up to our pumps. Wilbur just stared at both of us with his eyes bulging and his face red as a ripe tomato.

"Fill it with high-test, Son. Oh, and, good game last night," said Weems as he passed me.

"Yes sir. Thank you, sir," I said as I finished with Mr. Tiner's truck.

By the time I finished with the Olds, my uncle Neal had pulled up in his old green on green Bel-Air. He was my Dad's uncle and, being retired and a widower, came to the station most days just to hang around. If my Dad had errands to run, he left Uncle Neal in charge. I loved Uncle Neal. He always had great hunting and fishing stories and jokes that were what my Dad called "a little racy." But the jokes and stories were always funny.

As I entered the doorway, I heard Mr. Weems say, "Well, I see your gas went up a penny, but I forgot to look at Wilbur's sign. Has he caught up with you Big 'Un?"

"Oh, yeah," said Dad with a laugh. "What we got Dewey?"

"Two-fifty for Mr. Tiner, and $2.95 for Mr. Weems," I said.

Uncle Neal was at the window checking Wilbur's sign. "You know Big 'Un, I bet if you sold gas for a penny Wilbur'd give it away."

"Yeah," Dad laughed as he rang up the sales.

Mr. Weems finished a six-ounce Coke with one last gulp and, after a silent burp, said "You know, you could have some fun with him. You ought to change your price several times one day just to make Wilbur change his."

"Nahhh! I doubt he'd do that," said Dad. "He's pretty set in his ways, but he ain't crazy."

"Shoot! I bet he'd do it," said Mr. Tiner.

"Me, too," said Uncle Neal, "Dewey here could post the numbers, and me and you can change the pumps. Let's do it today just to aggravate that ole' cuss."

My dad looked across at Wilbur, who was reading the newspaper, while the other men laughed at their idea. "That might be fun at that," he mumbled to himself.

The next thing I knew, I was posting a price of twenty-three and nine. Dad decided we would only adjust the price for regular, so he changed the one pump, and we were set. We caught Wilbur by surprise. The newspaper had blocked his view. A good twenty minutes passed before he glanced toward us and then, upon turning away, whirled back around with those bulbous eyes looking as though they would burst.

Immediately he raced to his storeroom. Within minutes he was out front changing his sign and adjusting his pump. Those of us in the station giggled as we watched him scurry back into his station where he seemed to collapse in his chair, only to pop up once again to adjust the controls on his air-conditioners.

The price changes began to get people's attention. Over the next thirty minutes or so, three local cars and two cars of tourists stopped for gas. A couple of them passed the station then turned around and came back. I noticed that Wilbur had three customers during that time. All three cars had out-of-state tags.

When we finally reached a lull, Dad sent me out again to post a price of twenty-eight and nine, while Uncle Neal changed the pump. Wilbur had been standing before his window units. When he saw me heading for the sign, he literally jumped. I felt his eyes on me as I posted the new price. Within minutes Wilbur, his shirt soaked through with sweat, was out changing his prices.

When I got back inside, the men were doubled over laughing. "Did you see him jump?" howled Mr. Tiner. "Get a load of his shirt!" cried Uncle Neal. My dad just sat in his chair chuckling.

Mr. Weems had to leave, but he assured us he would return after lunch and made us promise to give him a detailed account of the day. Mr. Tiner, Uncle Neal, and Dad pulled Cokes out of the box. Uncle Neal drew Augusta, Georgia, and had to buy. Dad motioned for me to get one as well. I was glad. Before taking the first long swallow, I tilted my head back and held the ice-cold bottle to my throat. The chilled water running down my chest tickled its way across my belly to the top of my jeans.

About eleven o'clock that morning we moved our price back to twenty-six and nine, and Wilbur dutifully trudged out to go twenty-five and nine. Once back inside, I noticed Wilbur got a Coke out of the machine he kept at the station. By that time three or four other men had dropped by, saying that Mr. Weems had told them about "the game." Most of them indicated they would be back for the afternoon.

Shortly, Dad left to get our lunch. He went to an old-fashioned general store downtown and returned with a box of soda crackers, three cans of vienna sausage, and a hunk of hoop cheese. I loved those lunches with Dad and Uncle Neal. We watched as Wilbur got a Coke from his machine and sat down with the sandwich he always brought.

At Uncle Neal's urging, Dad had me go out and change our price again. I thought Wilbur would finish his sandwich, but, just as Uncle Neal had predicted, Wilbur dropped the sandwich and, after staring in disbelief until our numbers were posted, rushed to his storeroom and came out to change his price. Once back inside, I saw him get another Coke and again adjust his window units. After eating he went to his storeroom again. At first, I thought he was going to change his price yet again; instead he came back with a large window fan that he placed in front of his air conditioners.

Normally a hot Saturday afternoon would seem to last forever, but not this one. We never had less than five people in the station, most of whom came just to watch "the penny war" as they called it. We changed prices nine times that afternoon, usually because the crowd insisted that we do so.

Each time Wilbur followed suit, sweat pouring down his face, his shirt sticking to his back, his face as red as flame, and his eyes seeming to grow as the day went on. Wilbur bought half a dozen Cokes from his own machine. He apparently called and had his wife bring two more electric fans during the afternoon. Once in a while, he waited on a customer. The day was not particularly busy for either business—at least not as far as gas was concerned. I had to re-stock our drink box twice due to those men who came to watch.

They stayed an hour or so, spending most of the time laughing at and talking about "Ole' Wilbur." I noticed that my Dad got a little quieter as the day wore on. I figured he was simply growing bored with the whole thing. I knew I was.

At 5:30 Dad began urging the men to head on home. Some had livestock, and Dad would remind them of chores they had to "get done." For a couple, he merely had to ask what their wives had been doing that day; about the time their mouths dropped open, they were out the door. By ten minutes to six only Dad, Uncle Neal, and I were left. We prepared to close.

Uncle Neal laughed again and asked, "Gonna give Wilbur one more little nudge before we go Big 'Un?"

"Nahhh, I don't think so," my dad replied. He was about to say something else when Uncle Neal interrupted.

"Will you look at that?" I glanced up to see that all of the lights at Wilbur's had gone off. Wilbur came stomping out the door and looked around. Then he went back inside. We could see him turn on a flashlight and go over to his fuse box.

Uncle Neal howled with laughter again. "Hoo-wee, that fool's done blowed a fuse! Look-a-yonder. Ain't that something? I wish them other fellahs had stayed around to see this."

I started to laugh, but then I caught sight of my Dad's face. His expression was like a stone as he stared over at Wilbur. Without taking his eyes from the scene across the road he said, "Dewey, come here."

Wilbur was under his counter and therefore did not see me walk into his store. The yellow glow of the flashlight reflected off his bald head as he rummaged through the contents under the counter. I hesitated a bit and then, clearing my throat said, "Uh, Mr. Wilbur?"

"What? What is it?" he shouted, as his face snapped up toward me. The glow of the light and those huge, bulbous eyes frightened me for a moment. I almost dropped what I had in my hands. I stammered at first, "I . . . uh . . . I . . ."

"Well what is it? What do you want?" he said again. His face was in a scowl, and the sweat covered his forehead like a heavy dew with drops falling from the tip of his nose onto the counter.

Finally I recovered enough to say, "My Dad sent this . . ." On the counter I placed a couple of fuses and an ice cold bottle of Coke.

"I don't need . . ." Wilbur began, but then he flashed the light on the counter. Slivers of ice ran down the Coke bottle and already a puddle was forming on top of the counter. He looked at me, then walked over and peered out his window. My Dad was standing in his own doorway with a Coke in his hand. As Wilbur stared, Dad raised his bottle in a salute and held it there.

After what seemed a long time, Wilbur began to chuckle. He turned to the counter, and picking up the Coke I had brought, he walked to the door. As I went out past him, he raised the bottle in a return salute. The two men stood, each in his own entrance, holding their gestures to one another. As I walked away, Wilbur called out, "Tell your Dad I said 'I'm much obliged.' " The chuckle was still in his voice.

Food
for
Thought

"Did you say something?" My thoughts were preoccupied with wonder at the madness of Atlanta traffic. There were four lanes of traffic, and just ahead of us we could see the blockade that was forming. I wondered how much more this city could take. I loved Atlanta; I had since I was thirteen years-old and had spent a weekend vacation there with my family. Apparently, too many others had also fallen in love with our city.

Cassandra laughed, "Ah, already plotting your moves, eh." I winced to hear that she thought my mind was on work. My job was a good one, but very demanding. Business law attorneys make good money, in part, because the companies who hire them expect them to go wherever necessary and do whatever is needed (within the bounds of law and ethics—usually) to help the company succeed. As a lawyer, I struggled to maintain time for my wife and child but sometimes felt guilty, and this was one of those times.

I had had three days to prepare for a meeting in Washington with federal regulators, the bane of my existence. I would be there Friday and Saturday, returning home at mid-day on Sunday. I hated being away on the weekends. Raymond, the head of our legal department, always said, "With all the companies out there who invent loopholes and stretch and side-step the law, you would think the feds could cut some slack for companies that make every effort to comply." Then he would pause and say, "But then there was also a time when I believed in Santa Claus, the Easter Bunny, and Richard Nixon."

Suddenly, I realized I had still not responded to my wife's teasing. "Sorry, Cassie, I was just kind of transfixed by this traffic," I finally said.

"Yeah, right," she said with a roll of her eyes, "I take a half day to drive you to the airport, and you get absorbed by traffic." After the statement, she cut her eyes toward me with a half-smile to let me know she was teasing. Nevertheless, she had a point. Cassandra was a free-lance writer, which allowed her to work at home, and mornings were her most productive time. She really was going out of her way in driving me, so I bit the bullet and posed the question I had been considering for some time.

"Do you ever feel that you'd like to move?" I asked.

She chuckled and said, "Yeah, Paris would be nice, maybe Rome. Want me to call a real estate agent while you're gone?"

"No, I'm serious," I said. "I just wonder if the traffic and everything is worth it."

"Does 'everything' include the demands of your job?" She always did have a way of seeing right through me.

"Well, yes," I mumbled.

She reached over with a hand and squeezed my knee, "Oh, Ben, I know it's tough at times, and I do get frustrated with it occasionally, but we both love our work and Atlanta. Besides, you're pretty conscientious about taking time for me and Benji. He still hasn't stopped talking about last Wednesday."

A week ago Wednesday the Atlanta Braves played the Cincinnati Reds in an afternoon baseball game. The game started at 1:30, and I took the afternoon off to take Benji to the game. Our company had great box seats, and I had wrangled two tickets. I guess for an eight-year-old baseball fanatic like Benji, the day was like a dream. He even got autographs from several players.

The action was a spur-of-the-moment thing and somewhat out of character for me. I had obtained the tickets, thinking I would invite an attorney from one of our suppliers with whom we were trying to hammer out a new agreement. Halfway through the morning, however, I began thinking about Benji. I called, had Cassandra get him ready, and we made it to the park in time to eat hot dogs for lunch. I chuckled at the thought and told Cassandra, "Well, actually, I had as much fun as Benji."

She shook her head, "I don't know about that. Oh, I'm sure you enjoyed it, but Benji said it was the best day of his life." We both laughed at our son's flair for the dramatic.

Cassandra glanced at me as our lane of traffic slowed to a crawl. "Ben, tell me, what was the best day of your life when you were growing up?" she asked. I loved her off-the-wall question; in fact, I really envied that part of her personality.

I took a few minutes to think about her question. The worst day would have been easy to identify: when I was eighteen and my father died. Actually, I had never thought about the best day. When I was age twelve, my team won the local Little League championship. I had some good football and baseball games in high school. There were vacation days at the beach and that weekend trip to Atlanta. I had some good memories, but when I began to speak, I did not describe any of those times. In fact, I began to talk without having made a decision in my mind. I told of a day much earlier than high school—a day I had never dwelt on until my wife asked her specific question, a day that came back to me with remarkable clarity.

"Well, you know, my father was a salesman for the local grocery warehouse in town. He was on the road Monday through Friday, leaving by 7:00 A.M. and returning to the house anywhere from 6:00 to 8:00 P.M. I always loved to go with him in the summer, and he took me quite often. I loved the little stores we visited. In August of the summer when I was ten years-old, I went with him on a Tuesday. Tuesday was the day he stopped at my favorite place, Hamburg State Park—a wonderful place for a young boy.

"The park was near a virtual ghost town of a community named Jewell, on the banks of the Ogeechee River. The focal point was a good-sized lake filled with bream, catfish, and bass. A grist mill was built at the dam of the lake. The building was constructed in the early 1920s and, over the years, was maintained rather than modernized. Occasionally, I would get to go in the mill and see them grind the corn into meal.

"The lake was gorgeous and surrounded by trees. I loved to stand and watch the water rush over the dam to the spillway below. The spillway was a good place to fish for bream and catfish. A couple of Saturdays each year, my grandfather and I would ride up to Hamburg and fish the spillway and lake.

"An elderly couple named Hall ran a small country store there beside the lake. On this particular day we arrived at their store around 11:00 A.M., about an hour earlier than usual. I noticed that my dad had seemed to rush through some of his stops that morning, and I figured he was in a hurry to get home. Usually, he took a lot of time with most of his customers; many of them seemed to be more like old friends. Often, if the store owners were busy when my dad called on them, they would tell him to look around and write down what they needed. I was always amazed that they trusted him to know what they needed and knew he would not sell them something they could not use. If they were swamped with business, my dad would often pitch in and help them with their customers.

"Anyway, as we got to the store, we made our way up the wooden steps and through the screen door. As I said, the store was small—no more than fifteen feet by thirty feet. The entire structure was made of wooden boards, even the floor. In addition to corn meal ground at the old mill, the wooden shelves were stocked with canned goods, crackers, candy, cookies, tobacco products, and a few things like aspirin, insect repellant, and fishing tackle. I loved the floats and sinkers, hooks and lines, and plastic worms and artificial lures.

"There was an old ice box that contained chipped ice and soft drinks: Coca-Cola, Upper 10, Nehi Orange and Grape, Dr. Pepper, and Yoo-hoo chocolate drinks. When I pulled a drink out, cold water and ice slivers slid down the side, and I ran my hand down the bottle to knock off the water and ice before I removed the cap with the bottle opener on the front of the box.

"On the counter was a huge piece of cheese. My dad sold the cheese, which came in round, wooden boxes. The round flat hunk of cheddar, called hoop cheese, was coated with bright red wax; and thin, coarse, white cloth separated the cheese and wax. The Halls kept the cheese under a glass dome and cut it with a large butcher knife. Beside it was a roll of white butcher paper that was used to wrap the cheese.

"When we entered the store we heard the sound of hundreds of crickets. They were kept in a box along the back wall next to a refrigerator that stored worms—nightcrawlers, red-wigglers, and giant Louisiana pinks. Above the cricket box and the refrigerator were a huge bass and a large bream that had come out of the lake. The Hall's mounted them years ago. Hanging from the ceiling in front of the fish were two, huge, gray hornets' nests: they made me shudder when I saw them.

"Mrs. Hall was sitting in a rocker in front of the cricket box. Mr. Hall was on a stool behind the counter. 'Well, look who's here,' she said as she fanned herself with a cardboard funeral home fan.

" 'Hello, Ben, you're running ahead of schedule today. Hey there little Ben,' Mr. Hall said as I headed for the shelf with the fishing tackle. I don't remember the exact items the Halls ordered that day, but the remainder of the events are very clear now.

"As they were finishing business, and Mr. Hall was paying with cash for last month's orders, I pulled on my dad's pants pocket. I knew better than to interrupt while a customer was ordering. 'Daddy, can we eat here even though it's early?'

"My dad laughed and, as he rubbed his hand on my head, said, 'Sure son. Why don't you get what we need?' I knew exactly what to get: a can of vienna sausages, a small box of saltine crackers, a thick slice of hoop cheese, and two Coca-Colas.

"Mrs. Hall handed me the vienna sausages and the box of crackers. Then, she lifted the glass dome and, with the butcher knife, sliced a small, thin sliver of cheese for me to taste. The Halls always insisted that their customers taste the cheese before buying—I loved that. After I nodded, Mrs. Hall placed the dull, gray, knife blade just above the wax and waited for me to nod when the slice would be thick enough. I always got too much. Dad said my eyes were bigger than my stomach, but he never overruled me.

"While Mrs. Hall weighed and wrapped the cheese, I got two Cokes out of the ice box. As the water and ice slivers slid down the green glass sides, I held one to each of my cheeks to cool my face. I opened them and carried them to the counter.

"My dad paid the Halls, and we walked outside to one of the concrete picnic tables and benches under the pines between the store and the grist mill. From there I could see the lake, the top edge of the dam, and the back of the mill. The sun shone red-hot on the tin roof of the old mill and glinted off the surface of the water as it raced over the top edge of the dam. The pines and scattered sweet gums and willows on the opposite bank were a lush green. On our side, one large willow stretched its limbs over and down to the water. One of my favorite spots for bream was at the edge of those limbs.

"I watched as my dad took out his pocket knife to slice the cheese. He also used it to pull the sausages out of the can. We set them on the white butcher paper, and the jelled liquid held them in a clump. At that time of my life, it was my favorite meal. I would gladly have paid a large sum of money for that particular dining experience.

"As we ate we talked of fishing, baseball, and the impending start of school. My dad asked what I wanted to be when I grew up, a question he had asked thousands of times before. As always, I told him I was going to play second base for the New York Yankees. After all, Bobby Richardson wouldn't be able to play forever. At that age, the thought never occurred to me that I would not be good enough to play professional baseball—and my dad never made the suggestion to me.

"When we had finished eating, my dad carefully wiped his pocket-knife blade with his handkerchief. He always said a man ought to carry a good pocket knife. Then he told me to put our trash in the garbage can that was nearby. As I did, he headed back into the store. After depositing the trash, I sat and looked at the lake—the shimmering water broken occasionally by fish kissing the surface from beneath as they sought flies for their own meal. I closed my eyes and lay back on the concrete table, listening to the water as it poured over the dam and crashed to the rocks below.

"When I again opened my eyes, my dad was standing there, and I heard crickets. I saw that in his hands were two cardboard bait cups of worms and a cardboard box of crickets. 'Hold these,' he said.

"Still not sure what was going on, I watched as he went to the trunk of his car, opened it, and pulled out two rods and reels and a tackle box. I was excited as I said, 'Daddy, are we going to fish a while?'

"He laughed with that wonderful laugh of his and said, 'Son, we're going to fish the rest of the day!' And we did. He explained that he had called the rest of his customers at various points during the day and taken their orders over the phone. I asked him if any of them were mad that he wasn't coming by. He said he didn't think so. I asked what he told them for his excuse. He said he didn't need an excuse, that he told them he was taking his son fishing. Then I reminded him that in most stores he could look at the shelves and see things his customers needed but had not thought to order. I had seen him do this countless times. I asked if he wasn't losing money by not going to the stores. Even then I knew he worked, in part, for a commission. He laughed again and said somehow he didn't think he would miss whatever he might lose that afternoon.

"We fished all up and down the bank and in the spillway that afternoon. My dad told me about things he did when he was a boy. For the first time he told me how he and my mother started dating. He talked about his work and how much he liked what he did because of the people he met and those with whom he worked. He told me about playing football when he was in high school.

"For the first time I was able to ask my dad about something that had intrigued me since the first of the year. One night in January a man who owned a small department store in our town had come to our house. He and my dad had gone into our living room and had talked for over an hour. My mother had always avoided any questions I had posed about that evening.

"My dad smiled and thought for a moment, then told me that the man had offered him a job helping run a new store in another town. My dad said he had told the man 'no,' even when he kept trying to talk my dad into taking the job. I asked if the other job would have paid more and my dad said, 'yes.'

"Then I asked why he had turned down the offer. He said, 'It was a matter of loyalty.' I asked what he meant, and he said when he and my mom had moved to our town he did not have a job and was right out of the army. The people at the grocery warehouse gave him a job—first in the warehouse and later promoted him to sales. He said he felt he 'owed them something.'

"Funny, I loved to fish then, and I remember what we talked about, but I can't remember much about what we caught. There were a few bream, maybe a couple of catfish, and a bass, I think. Anyway, Dad borrowed a knife from the Halls and cleaned the fish, then packed them in ice from the drink box to take home. We ate more cheese and crackers on the way."

As I finished my story, I noticed Cassandra was turning off the interstate. She was smiling but seemed unable to speak. I glanced out the window then practically yelled, "Quick, turn right."

As I found my seat on the plane, I put my briefcase into the overhead storage, then sat down with my brown paper sack. A fiftyish-looking man sat next to me. After our departure, my neighbor stared at me in disbelief as I took from the bag saltine crackers, a wedge of cheese, and a can of vienna sausages. Finally the man said, "What's the matter, airline food disagree with you?"

I chuckled as I reached for my pocket knife. "No," I said, "but right now, I'm feeding a memory."

Miss Mamie's Boys

I had to admit I was impressed with what I was seeing. A crowd that I judged to number over 10,000 had gathered for the Cooperative Baptist Fellowship's annual meeting, the first I had attended. I was struck by the warmth and enthusiasm I witnessed. This was the night of the missions emphasis and, try as I might, I could not help but reminisce about the person who taught me what little I do know about missions: Miss Mamie Lee Hayes.

In the small Georgia town in which I was raised, the Baptist church was the center of cultural and social life for many folks. Just about everyone I knew was at the church on Sunday morning. Quite a few people were there on Sunday night, and somewhere in-between the attendance at those times was the group that gathered on Wednesday for the family night covered dish supper and the missions organizations.

Although no one would have admitted it, most of the ladies viewed these suppers as a contest. Each one tried to outdo the other with the dishes she brought. I remember the serving tables piled high with platters of crispy fried chicken and homemade biscuits. There were dozens of casseroles: macaroni and cheese, broccoli, squash, chicken, and any other type you could imagine. The desserts were out of this world—pies and cakes, cookies and, my favorite, banana pudding.

As I said, no one would admit to the contest, but I do remember the two or three times that my mother's Wednesday night dish did not "turn out right." She suddenly took ill and could not make it to church. On those occasions, she sent me, my dad, and my older sister on with a bowl of peas or corn from the freezer.

Once I was old enough to realize what was going on with the contest, I enjoyed getting to the fellowship hall early so that I could watch people enter. Every woman carefully examined the other dishes on the table, trying to decide the best positioning for her own dish. I eventually discovered that no one wanted her dish next to Gerald Turner's.

Mr. Turner's wife died at an early age and, in raising two children, he was forced to learn to cook. The man learned well. His casseroles were always perfect. When he made an asparagus casserole, even the children ate it. Of course, this infuriated our mothers who could never get us to eat asparagus at home. Every woman in our church knew that if her food were next to Mr. Turner's food, his dish would overshadow hers, and she avoided his dish like the plague.

My habit of getting inside early facilitated my first encounter with Miss Mamie Lee Hayes. On one particular Wednesday when I was nine years-old, I was feeling sharp pangs of hunger. Lunch at school that day had been particularly discolored and unappetizing, and temptation was great. As I watched dish after dish being brought in, the hollow pit in my stomach grew larger and larger.

At one point I found myself alone in the fellowship hall and, oddly enough, close to the dessert table. Miss Hayes had brought in a pile of brownies earlier. They were dark and rich with chocolate, interrupted by occasional spots of marshmallow. Slowly and deftly I eased my hand under the plastic wrap dome that covered them. The rustle of the wrap allowed the escape of a heavenly aroma of chocolate. Just as I eased a brownie to the edge of the wrap, I heard a voice behind me saying, "Don't you dare!"

I was so startled that I attempted to jerk my hand away, but the wrap held tight, and the move resulted in the whole plate of brownies being dumped into the floor. I turned to see the imposing figure of Miss Hayes staring at me, with her hands on her hips. I was so frightened I could not speak. I believe her initial silence was more the result of surprise or shock.

After what seemed an eternity, she launched into a speech. Later I remembered only one part of what she said, but the one part would be forever imbedded in my memory. She said that she had a nephew overseas in India, and in that country, stealing could get your hand cut off. I think I ran off with my mouth and eyes still wide open. Later, my parents learned of the incident and made me apologize to her. She accepted the apology but still scared me. In the weeks to come, I discovered that most of my friends had some type of terrifying encounter with this woman at some point in their lives. Judging from the way Mom and Dad talked about that night, when they thought I was not listening, they were not real comfortable around the woman either.

I am not sure which of my friends coined the phrase, but soon Miss Hayes came to be known by my group of friends as "The Old Battle Ax." Now, none of us really knew what a battle ax was, and certainly none of us had ever seen such a thing, but somehow the word had the right ring to it when it was applied to Miss Mamie Lee Hayes. We decided that, all in all, it must be a fitting name. Imagine, then, the combination of terror, confusion, and impending sense of doom we experienced when we learned, the following fall, that our new R.A. leader would be none other than the battle ax herself.

Our group consisted of ten boys ranging in age from nine to eleven. I was ten years-old at the time. From what we could piece together, primarily by listening carefully when our parents were sure we were "otherwise occupied," we had simply worn out our old R.A. leader, Mr. Bailey. We were a rambunctious group at times, and it was difficult for us to sit and listen to him read out of the missions magazine. Mr. Bailey was in his sixties and apparently decided he was ready for retirement as an R.A. leader, even if he was still able to run his gas station six days a week.

Evidently our group had quite a reputation, because, according to our parents, the preacher had trouble recruiting another leader. Miss Hayes, as the perennial president of the Woman's Missionary Union, felt it her calling to provide the preacher with the "encouragement" necessary to keep the search going to a successful conclusion. Toward the end of the summer, the preacher had apparently gotten all the encouragement he could stand and, in essence, told Miss Hayes that if she was so interested in the class maybe *she* should teach it.

Now, I always liked Reverend Wells, and I think he kind of liked me and my friends. I have to believe that he never really thought Miss Hayes would take him up on his offer but, much to our dismay, she did. Reverend Wells was a smart man and decided not to tell us in advance about our new leader.

The first Wednesday night of the fall, we were gathered in our appointed room playing marbles on the floor. Fortunately, we had discovered we could make our ring on the short-pile rug with a piece of chalk. Travis Dunbar and Greg White got into an argument over something, and we were all putting in our two cents' worth when the door swung wide, and we saw the battle ax standing there. At first it did not bother us so much, for we were under the mistaken impression that this room was still our turf. In our minds we had home-field advantages, for she had wandered into our territory. Little did we know a coup had taken place.

When Miss Hayes slammed the door and cleared her throat, she got our attention. "Boys," she said, "what is the R.A. motto?"

Well, we had all heard it before, but that had been a while back and, basically, we were in a temporary state of shock. We sat there wide-eyed with our mouths open.

"Oh, come on," she said as she moved around the room, "You are Royal Ambassadors. Where did you get that name?"

I really did remember the motto; I just could not force my mouth to work. Apparently, neither could anyone else.

"Alright, have a seat," Miss Hayes said as she walked over to the board. We all scrambled, leaving our marbles on the floor. She wrote on the board, "We are ambassadors for Christ. II Corinthians 5:20." Then she said, "You will learn this by next week, and I assure you we will recite it each time we meet." Then she began to tell us what missionaries did and how her nephew was called to the mission field and how the Southern Baptist Convention's Foreign Missions Board had helped him get there.

At one point, Travis and Greg started whispering to one another. After all, their dispute had been interrupted. Without changing tone, Miss Hayes circled around behind them, moving ever so slowly and deliberately. She reminded me of a "Wild Kingdom" episode I had seen where Marlin Perkins filmed a mountain lion stalking a deer. The deer never saw the lion, just as Travis and Greg never saw Miss Hayes. They felt her, though, as she thumped the backs of their ears with her middle fingers. I cringed when they yelled because I knew how much it hurt. "Remember boys, when you use your ears the way you are supposed to use them, they won't hurt," Miss Hayes said, "and right now you are supposed to be listening to me." We all sat terrified but very attentive for the rest of the lesson.

We were determined we would not go down without a fight. Travis and Dub Brown, the oldest ones in the group, declared they would not come back. There was no way their parents would make them put up with the battle ax. Greg started to say something, then rubbed his ear and changed his mind. By the following Sunday it became apparent that we had no recourse. Our fates were sealed; our hides belonged to the battle ax.

One thing we learned right away was that Miss Hayes would not read to us out of the missions magazine. She had a lot of contact with her nephew, and she told us stories about his work and the work of others. She also made us do things.

One night she took us to old Mr. Wiggins' farm and had us carry water from his creek to a cistern beside his barn. The whole time she was telling us how far some people in other countries had to walk to get water. Then she told us how important it was to have money and missionaries who could design and build water pumps and irrigation systems.

One night she would not let us eat in the fellowship hall. Instead, she gave each of us a small bowl of plain rice and dared us to snack when we got home. There was no chance of that anyway because she had talked to our parents. The lesson was on hunger, and we all developed a much greater appreciation for the hungry people in the world.

The next week she talked about the work of the Southern Baptist Convention's Home Mission Board and mentioned the poor in America. Travis, having grown bold and forgotten about his ear, spoke up and said, "Aw, there ain't no poor people in America, just folks that's too lazy to work." Miss Hayes' response was an icy glare. Before we knew it, she had us in her car (all ten of us) headed for the part of our town that was known as Jenkins' Alley. All of us had been warned by our parents never to go near that section of town; and she not only drove us there, but she made us get out.

The sun was going down as we walked behind her—all of us huddled into one frightened, quivering, mass of naivety. We saw dirty children in ragged clothes. Almost all of them were barefoot, which we would not have minded ourselves had the ground not been so covered with broken glass and rusted nails and cans. We saw food tossed out in the yard instead of thrown into a garbage can, the scraps fought over by thin, mangy-looking dogs. We saw front porches that had collapsed and windows filled with cardboard or jagged pieces of broken glass. Doors were half on and half off their hinges. Miss Hayes took us right up to one of those doors.

She knocked, and a voice inside said, "Come in." We entered, still holding on to one another. One bare light bulb, hanging by a fraying cord in the middle of the room, illuminated the interior. The place smelled of old smoke and sweat. The floor was a jigsaw puzzle of rotted boards and soiled linoleum. A rusted iron bed, a low table with three legs, a couch with no cushions, an arm chair, and three splintered wooden chairs were all of the furniture. The walls were brown and stained, with several newspaper patches. There were two pictures on the wall. One was of the face of Jesus, and the other was a crudely framed magazine cover of Martin Luther King, Jr.

In the arm chair sat an old, white-haired, black woman. Her skin reminded me of my mother's coffee after she added milk in the mornings. The woman had no teeth. She sat wrapped in a dingy, yellow bathrobe, her gnarled toes peeking out from slippers that looked to be falling apart before our very eyes. Her eyes were strange. They were not as dark as I had expected. Instead, they were kind of white-looking, even in the middle.

"Aunt Mattie," Miss Hayes said, "I've brought some boys to pick up your yard." And pick up we did as the old black woman sat on the collapsing porch talking to Miss Hayes. We learned that Aunt Mattie was eighty-seven years-old and blind. We saw the three great-grandchildren, all younger than us, that she was raising. We learned that she had not heard from their mother in two years—right after the youngest one's birth. I remember thinking that I never knew people could live like this.

In the winter Miss Hayes arranged for our group to go coon hunting. She got Mr. Wilbur Street to bring his dogs and a twenty-two rifle. She told us whatever we got that night would be taken to Aunt Mattie because she would cook and eat it. For a while all of us were afraid she would make us eat with Aunt Mattie.

None of us had ever been coon hunting before. We had a wonderful time chasing the dogs through the woods. We killed one coon and a possum pretty quickly when the dogs treed a third time. Shining his flashlight up in the trees, Mr. Wilbur finally found two greenish eyes up near the top of the oak at which we were gathered. The dogs were in a frenzy around the base of the trunk. With Joey Monroe having been given the high honor of holding the light, Mr. Wilbur fired the rifle. Joey followed the carcass as it tumbled down from limb to limb.

I guess it dawned on all of us at the same time that we were seeing not brown or grey fur but fur that was black and white, black and white, black and white. By the time the form reached the lower limbs, our brains engaged our mouths and, in unison, we yelled, "Skunk!" We promptly scattered to the four corners of the earth. The dogs were not so quick-witted. For the rest of the night we did not have to see or hear the dogs to know where they were. This was the first time we saw Miss Hayes laugh. In the past we had caught a few brief glimpses of smiles, but never had we heard a chuckle, but now we wondered if she would ever stop laughing.

In the spring, Miss Mamie had us plant small gardens in four places around our town. At first we thought she had indeed gone crazy. One area was an old road bed. Another area was filled with rocks. A third plot was in the midst of some blackberry vines. Only one of the gardens was in a decent spot.

Then she told us Jesus' parable about the sower. She told us people were like those types of ground and what a challenge that presented for missionaries trying to plant the seed of the gospel in the hearts of those folks. Then she reminded us that in some parts of the world people had no other kind of soil and that, unlike us, those people could not run to the Winn-Dixie store when they wanted a tomato sandwich. We tended what grew in our good garden and gave the vegetables to Aunt Mattie.

Somewhere along the way, our fear of Miss Mamie turned into respect. We began to look forward to R.A.'s each Wednesday. She stayed with us through high school. Four of us were on the football team in tenth grade. One Wednesday the coach worked the team late, and we walked off the field so we could make it to Pioneers—as we were then called. The coach told us we would be kicked off the team, but we went anyway. Oddly enough, after Miss Mamie visited the coach at school the next day, we found we were still on the team and never again did we practice late on Wednesdays.

In time, respect turned into love for Miss Mamie, love for the poor and the lost, and love for each other. I guess Miss Mamie loved us too. She died a few years back, and we were all there for her funeral. We came from many places. We learned that each of us is actively involved in our local churches and communities helping others and teaching children and youth as well as adults.

The nephew who had been a missionary in India was there too. He told us of the thousands of questions Miss Mamie used to ask in her letters—questions about missions that would help her with her "little group of R.A.'s" as she called us. He said he believed he detected a change in her after she began teaching us, as though she had begun to enjoy life again for the first time since the accident that claimed her husband at an early age and caused her miscarriage. We were stunned. None of us had ever known she had been married, much less that she had suffered a miscarriage.

My thoughts were interrupted by the realization that the missions emphasis was drawing to a close. We were invited to walk down to the floor of the arena and speak to the missionaries who were being commissioned. I moved to the aisle, along with eight others of our original group of ten people. Only Travis was not with us. Instead, he was already down on the floor. The year before he had given up his law practice so that he and his wife could lead a mission in India.

As we reached the floor, I grabbed Travis first as we surrounded him, his wife, and two children. We laughed as I said, "Don't you wish Miss Mamie could see this."

Travis put his hands on my shoulders and with a smile said, "To tell you the truth, guys, I'm convinced that right now somewhere she and Aunt Mattie are sitting on a sturdy, new porch in comfortable rocking chairs celebrating with us."

Bubba Explains

My name is Bubba Miller, and I play football—because it's there. I'm six-feet-two and weigh 235 pounds—before breakfast. I scratch where I itch and ain't never said "sir" to nobody since my daddy died when I was twelve. I don't drink, smoke, or cuss unless it's absolutely necessary—and I'm out of ear-shot of children, preachers, and my third grade teacher, Miss Dillehaw.

What I'm about to tell you happened last night. Right now, it's 3:00 A.M., and I'm sitting on the front porch of our house. I'm in a rocking chair, and I swear I'm going to keep rocking until I understand all of this.

Now the biggest worry someone like me ought to have on the night of the homecoming football game of his senior year is how many bones he can break of the other team's quarterback and where he ought to go parking with his girlfriend when the dance is over. In fact, if I made a mistake this particular night, as near as I can figure, it was in not giving enough thought to the second thing I just mentioned. How one decision caused the mess that followed is weird, but I think all of it somehow fits together.

There was nothing unusual about yesterday morning. Any day at Haney High School is about as dull as any other. By the time you reach twelfth grade, even the fifth-period pep rally and the useless sixth-period class that follows are routine. The band played something that sounded like "Theme on a Hog Stuck in a Culvert." The cheerleaders did a skit that made sense only to them, and jumped around, yelling and showing us their underwear.

I never could figure why the same girl who slapped you in second period because she thought you were leaning out of your desk so you could look up her dress (when all you were doing was picking up your pencil from the floor) was so all fired-up about you seeing her underwear while she was cheerleading during fifth period. Of course, I guess she may have been wondering how some guy who hangs onto a football while eleven crazy boys try to separate him from it has so much trouble holding a number-two pencil while he's writing.

Anyway, the coach mumbled the same speech he always does at pep rallies, which is basically his pre-game and half-time speech

without all the cussing and locker-kicking. Then he called the cap-
tains—me and Frog Harley and Red Willis—out on the gym floor
and told us to tell the rest of the school what we were going to do
to the Pine County Red Raiders. Just like always, Frog told the
team he was going to grab that microphone and say right out,
"We're gonna beat the hell out of 'em!" But, as usual, he wound
up saying we were going to "run the crossbuck play, because nobody could beat the blocking on the crossbuck play." All of the
cheerleaders yelled and screamed, even though none of them knew
a crossbuck play from a cross-your-heart bra.

After the pep rally, we all went to our sixth-period class where
the only thing anybody learned was who didn't have a date for the
dance. Of course, if you were one of those who didn't, what you
learned in sixth period could have a dramatic effect on your life,
at least for the rest of Friday. During the sixth-period class on
homecoming day, I made the fateful decision to drive Tammy to
Puckett's Lake after the dance.

Puckett's Lake is seven-and-a-half acres of water, surrounded
by trees off Old Saw Mill Road. The things that make this lake
ideal for parking are: (1) On either side of the dam are clearings
large enough for ten or twelve cars or trucks; and (2) There are
three entrances to the dam area, and the county sheriff knows that
people who go there have something on their minds other than
speeding, shooting road signs, or stealing bales of hay—which
means he leaves those people alone until 2:00 A.M. or so.

The thing that made Puckett's Lake ideal for me was that Frog,
Red, and I found a trail leading down by the creek below the dam
—a trail that no one else seemed to know about (or so we thought
at the time), a trail that was big enough for my truck and too muddy for anything without oversized tires and four-wheel drive.

I finalized my decision during sixth period because my teacher,
Mrs. Alberson, sent me to the shop building to tell Mr. Russell that
her pencil sharpener was loose again. Mrs. Alberson usually sent
me because she was Tammy's mother, and she liked the idea of
Tammy going out with me. I was always respectful of her and
Tammy, which apparently was more than she got from her ex-
husband. The errand gave me an opportunity to check the consistency of the mud on the dirt road that circled the back of the

school. I found the mud to my liking because the rain of the past week had left it so that my tennis shoes made a soft popping sound as they came out of it—perfect mud for my truck with its oversized tires.

The consistency factor of the mud was vitally important, for Tammy and I needed to be undisturbed last night. Although Tammy did not know it, I planned to present her with my class ring. It was a shining oval, whose value was determined more by its die-cast surface than the gold—if it really was gold—that went into it. On one side was the proud horseshoe, the symbol of the Haney High School Colts, and on the other side were the initials HHS and the year, 1988. The blue stone on top was more valuable than a sapphire to me, for it was one of our school colors. The design beneath the stone, which the salesman identified as a sunburst, was carefully selected as my own individual touch for the symbol of my high school days.

I wore the ring the previous spring and summer and was prepared to present it to Tammy as undeniable proof of my loyalty to her. An engagement ring could not have said more about my feelings for her. Anyone with a few hundred dollars can buy an engagement ring, but my class ring was earned through four years of successful toil and triumph over such inhumane tribulation as chemistry, world literature, algebra, and study hall with "the whispering dragon" (our name for the school librarian, Mrs. Cooper).

Well, as it turned out, Frog should have said we'd beat the hell out of the Red Raiders because that's exactly what we did—exactly what you're supposed to do at your homecoming game. I guess I got a little sentimental or something in light of my later plans. I play linebacker, and I normally count on planting the butt of the other team's quarterback pretty early in a game. Last night, though, we were up 21–0 before I even had a shot at him, and I decided (out of the goodness of my heart) to let him live.

Halfway through the fourth quarter, we were ahead 42–0 when the other team's quarterback did a stupid thing: He scored a touchdown from a trick play. Even though our scrubs were in on defense, the coach had set his heart on a shut-out, and the touchdown kinda' got to him. Then when those idiots lined up to go for a two-point conversion, he cussed, threw his cap, and made our guys call a time-out. Then he told the first team defense to go back in, and that just burned my butt.

With five minutes left in the third quarter, we came out for what we were sure would be the last time for the game. Since it was homecoming, some of us had already cut the tape off our ankles and wrists so we would be able to get out of the locker room much faster. Now, I could just see me twisting an ankle, or spraining a wrist, or worse, and spending time in the hospital on what was would be the most important night of my life—not to mention Tammy's life. So, on the way out on the field, I made up my mind that the opposing quarterback would pay for this one.

We knew the other team would try to pass the ball since its players hadn't been able to run all night. In the huddle, I called our defense and told them the quarterback was mine. When the ball was snapped, I found a huge gap in the line. As soon as I got through it, I saw the quarterback's eyes. There was a lot of white in them. The last time I had seen eyes like that was when the high beams on my truck caught a deer on Highway 221. I think I was doing sixty-five and slowed down a lot by the time I hit it. I didn't slow down for the quarterback, though.

I knew he had thrown the ball away, hoping the act would protect him and, according to the rules, it should have. Well, so much for rules. Once he threw the ball, he was just like the deer: He stood there, waiting for the truck. The license number for this one was forty-two, and it was on the front and back—of my jersey. His number was fifteen. I've always hated numbers that begin with one. I put the front of my helmet between the one and five, knowing it would slide up his chest and catch his chin. My forearms caught his stomach. I could hear the air explode from his lungs before he hit the ground. I never lost my footing.

I wound up standing over him with a foot on either side of his chest. His eyes were still wide open, and so was his mouth as he gasped and wheezed in an effort to get his breath back. The blood on his chin quickly spread. I never said a word to him—I never do; I just look at them until their eyes focus on mine, then I walk away. Before he could focus, though, I saw the referee's yellow flag float between us to land on his chest. I heard the ref say "That's 'Roughing the Passer' number forty-two."

He saw me, so I looked at the ref as I turned and said, "Yeah, you got that right." They helped number fifteen off the field, and number twelve came on—he was even more of a wimp. I just stared at him as he came to the line; I knew I had him. He was so busy looking for me he never saw Red coming at him from defensive end. Red went kind of easy on him, and we all trotted to the side-line. The coaches gave me a 9.9 on the hit. I asked why it wasn't a ten, and they said, "Because he got up." We won 49-6.

By eleven o'clock I was showing my moves on the gym floor. I could do alright dancing, even though I'd skip dances if it weren't for Tammy. She loves that stuff, and I have to admit her moves just about drive me crazy. She's got this slow, slinky kind of move that causes her dark hair to fall over her dark eyes. Then those eyes kind of peek up at me, and she flashes this huge smile —all white teeth and dimples. While I'd never tell her this, once she flashes that smile, I'm as helpless as a chicken with its head on the chopping block. She was flashing it a lot last night.

The dance was to last until 12:30 A.M., but most of the team and their dates left at midnight so that we could go by Minnie's to eat. Most of us have grown up eating at Minnie's, and we eat there after every home football game. Everybody has their own place to sit. Seniors and their dates get the booths. The younger ones get the tables. Tammy and I slid into our corner booth and waited for Edna to get to us.

Edna has been at Minnie's as long as we can remember. We give her a hard time, but she usually gives it right back to us. She came to our booth and asked "What'll it be, Bubba?"

I suppose I was being kind of a smart-aleck when I said, "Oh we'll have the roast duck with orange sauce."

Edna gave me a look that said, "You're exactly what I need at midnight on Friday."

I laughed and said, "Hamburger steak, fries, and a Coke." I always order the same thing, as do most of the rest of the guys.

As she wrote my order, she said with a straight face, "Well I wasn't sure you were yourself tonight, Bubba. I understand the quarterback got up."

She had me. Even Tammy had to giggle a bit, but she quickly recovered and ordered french fries and a salad.

Tammy kept asking why I was eating so fast. I lied and said it was because I was starving. Actually, I just wanted to get away from the crowd as quickly as possible. Of course, I couldn't tell her that. She wasn't the kind of girl who would be flattered to hear that a guy just wanted to get her alone, and I couldn't risk tipping her off about my plans for the evening.

I never knew it could take so long to eat a salad and a few french fries, but, at last, Tammy finished. From my perspective, I thought I waited forever before speaking. In reality I said, "Wanna go for a ride?" about the time her knife and fork hit her plate.

She kind of sighed and leaned back, letting her eyes wander around the room. Then she said, "Oh, I don't know. Maybe we should listen to the juke box and visit with some of the others."

I was about to bust, and before she had a chance to flash me those dimples and let me know she was teasing, I blurted out, "I've got a stereo in the truck and, besides, ain't nobody here but dumb football players and their flirty, cheerleader girlfriends."

When she laughed I knew I'd been had and laughed myself. Then I threw some money on the table and we left.

When I started slowing down, as we approached Puckett's Lake, Tammy went back to her routine. "Why, Bubba" (the way she said my name was so sweet it sounded as though it was bubbling up out of a vat of honey), "whatever do you think we would do here when it's so late and so dark?"

"Perfect conditions for watching the submarine races, my dear," I said while making the turn. That was an old joke in our town. One of our teachers, who was a Yankee and about as naive as a Church of God preacher, once heard us refer to submarine races and said, "Why boys, I don't understand. There are no submarines around here. And, even if there were, you could hardly watch them race, particularly at night. Why you might as well be sitting there in the dark."

We seemed to be the first ones there, which I had counted on. I drove through the clearing where we normally parked and turned on my high beams so I could find the path at the back. Tammy asked, "Where we going, Bubba?" as she slid closer to me on the seat.

She wasn't worried. She drove me wild most of the time, and I got the feeling she felt pretty strongly about me, but she knew she was safe. We usually just sat there a lot, listening to music and planning our future. I let others think whatever they wanted to think. They had seen me bust up too many guys on the football field to say whatever they were thinking.

I found the path beside a pine tree that has a big knot about seven feet up its trunk. I then rolled through the brush into the tiny clearing on the other side of the stand of pines. I went a couple of hundred yards down the path before I stopped.

When I looked at Tammy, I thought maybe she *was* worried. So, before she could say anything, I said "Relax, I just thought there might be a big crowd out there tonight, and some of those fools will be drinking, and I just didn't feel like busting up any aggravating drunks tonight." She seemed to relax and put her head on my shoulder and turned up the stereo.

We listened to music and talked for a while. I kept waiting for just the right moment—the right lead-in. We covered the game, the dance, which guys were with which girls, and some school stuff. Then Tammy took my right hand from her shoulder, kissed it, and said, "I'm glad you found this spot, Bubba; it is nice not to worry about Ricky and Maggie getting in a fight and disrupting things."

Ricky and Maggie fight about every other weekend. Twice we have driven Maggie home. One Saturday we drove Ricky home when he passed out on the hood of my truck. I wanted to tie him to the front bumper, but Tammy protested; so we compromised, and I dumped him in the back. Of course, I didn't tell Tammy I had spent the day hauling compost for my mama's flower beds. I believe Ricky became aware of the fact when he regained consciousness on Sunday morning. In fact, the odor may have helped bring him around.

Tammy was squeezing my hand with the class ring, so it seemed like the right time. I withdrew my arm and said as I started to take it off, "Tammy I want you to have this."

The look in her eyes was unbelievable—soft, far-away, moist, and excited. The evening was turning out even better than I had hoped. She had just managed to sigh, "Oh, Bubba . . .," when we heard the first shot.

BOOM! I figured it must be a twelve-gauge. I thought it was somebody hunting until I heard the sharp crack of a pistol and then another. Immediately I turned off the stereo and rolled down my window; I could hear people in the woods.

BOOM! Tammy screamed and covered her ears. Then I heard, "Hey, Slim, they're heading up the path to the lake."

Somebody answered, "Don't get too close, Buck; they've still got their guns." I looked at Tammy at the same time her wide-open eyes and mouth turned to me. We both knew Slim and Buck were the sheriff's deputies who worked our end of the county. The thought flashed through my mind that two prisoners had escaped from the county jail last month and still hadn't been caught.

I cranked the truck with one hand and rolled up the window with the other. Tammy was screaming, "Bubba, oh Bubba, what are we gonna do?" I didn't have time to answer. I shifted into reverse, put my arm on the seat behind her, half turned my upper body, and floored the accelerator. The path was wide enough to back up with speed until we reached the clearing. Once there, I slammed on the brakes while cutting the wheels hard to the left. Frog, Red, and I call this a "bat-turn." I executed it as flawlessly as I did the blitz on the extra-point play. The truck spun 180 degrees in the middle of the muddy path. Once it stopped, I shifted into first and turned on my headlights as I floored the accelerator a second time.

Then I hit the brakes again—real hard. Tammy was thrown to the floor board. She screamed again and yelled, "Bubba, what's wrong?" Clawing at the dash, she pulled herself up until she saw what I saw. A pine tree had fallen across the path. I didn't panic —yet. As quickly as possible I started circling the little clearing with my high-beams on, looking for an opening. Only after the second circuit did it register with me that I had seen, out of the corner of my eye, an axe imbedded in the stump of the downed tree. Somebody was playing a trick on us.

When I stopped, the truck was pointing back down the path. I heard the pistols fire again and heard the voices, although I couldn't make out the words. I rolled my window down and put a hand over Tammy's mouth. "Shhh! Listen," I whispered.

They were still coming up the path, making a lot of noise. Then I heard, "Careful, Slim; they'd just as soon shoot as look at you!" The voice belonged to Ricky. I was mad. I released Tammy and gripped the steering wheel. Without looking at Tammy, I said, "Buckle up." I did the same myself as she reached for the seat belt.

Tammy looked at me and said, "But what . . .," and her words were left hanging in the air as I hit the gas. We were flying down the path, bouncing on the seat as the beams of the lights bobbed ahead of us.

"Hang on," I said as I caught a glimpse of a figure ahead. The light beams came down out of the limbs again, and I caught a fleeting look at the face as he dove out of the way and dropped the pistol. The face belonged to Ricky alright. I couldn't recognize the other two persons, but one had a pistol and the other had a shotgun. I sped through them, hoping my tires were throwing a ton of mud on top of them as we continued down the path.

In a moment, I slowed a little and let out a long sigh. Tammy was staring straight ahead, but she did manage to mumble, "Who was that?"

"Barf-breath Ricky and a couple of his drunken pals," I grunted between clinched teeth. "I promise they'll pay—but later."

"Oh, forget it," Tammy said, finally relaxing her grip on the door arm rest, "let's just get out of here."

I knew the path followed Brier Creek until it came out on 221 at the county line bridge. I think I increased my speed a bit as I began to explain to Tammy. "Those guys must have been waiting on us. I'll bet Ricky heard Frog and Red talking about this path in biology. We found this trail a month or so ago when we were scouting for spots for our deer stands. I told them to keep their mouths shut, but I bet Ricky overheard them. He and the other guys chopped down the tree then must have circled through the woods to come up in front of us like that. I gotta hand it to . . ."

All I remember was a blur of red, then I saw my high beams flashing up in the trees as Tammy screamed yet again. Coming down was like being in a slow-motion replay. I remembered seeing films of games when I hit guys, and they came down just like that —slow, but hard.

Maybe I was knocked out for a minute. The next thing I remembered was thinking how quiet it was. I heard moans and looked at Tammy. She was conscious, and her mouth was open as she stared at me, but the moans didn't seem to be coming from her. I noticed that the windshield on my truck was shattered. I thought it was strange that my hood wasn't crumpled. In fact, I couldn't remember seeing anything we could have hit, plus I had the weird sensation of floating. I asked Tammy if she was O.K., and she said she was.

I opened the door to see the damage, and the ground wasn't there. I grabbed the armrest on the door and found the ground with my feet. I heard the same moan again and saw something red under my truck. If I hadn't seen it, I wouldn't have believed it. My truck was sitting on top of a car.

"Bubba?" It was Tammy.

"Hang on," I said as I made my way around to her side. I could tell someone was in the car—maybe even two people. The roof was smashed in pretty good. I helped Tammy down and told her we were on top of a car. "Oh, oh, Bubba," she said.

The car was really flattened, and there was a lot of broken glass. I reached in through a small space where a window used to be. There was no more than six inches of an opening. I felt what seemed to be an arm. "Help!" someone in the car yelled. I tried the door, but it wouldn't budge.

I yelled, "Wait a minute, let me try the other side." This door was jammed too, and there was definitely more than one person in there. The same one spoke again.

"Can't you do something?" a woman's voice pleaded—a voice that was somehow familiar.

Tammy made a sound as though she was sucking in a roomfull of air and said, "Mother?"

"What?" came the voice from the car.

Tammy leaned over the hood of the car and looked in. Sure enough—there was Mrs. Alberson! I could see that she and the other person were both in the passenger's seat. She was in the other person's lap, although they were both bent over toward the middle of the car.

At that point, the other person groaned and raised his head a bit from behind Mrs. Alberson. "Why, Mr. Russell," I said, "hey, you O.K. in there?"

Mr. Russell groaned again and mumbled, "Yeah, I think so."

"Well good," I said, greatly relieved, "because I can't get the doors open, and I don't think you've got room to crawl out. I believe I'm going to have to go for help."

"Do what!?!" yelled Mrs. Alberson.

"Get help," I said. "Don't you think so Tammy?"

Tammy didn't answer. She had her hands over her mouth and a wild-eyed look about her. She didn't seem to be able to speak.

I heard a lot of grunting and groaning inside the car. Mr. Russell and Mrs. Alberson were trying to move something inside so they could get more room or maybe even get out. But I could already tell the situation was hopeless.

I couldn't figure out why Tammy seemed so surprised. Her mother was divorced; Mr. Russell and his wife were separated and on the way to a divorce. Most folks in town suspected that the two of them had something going on. People talked about it, but no one seemed upset about it. I had even figured that the pencil sharpener deal was some kind of a signal. No pencil sharpener tore up as much as Mrs. Alberson's. I kind of figured the two of them had been pretty open with this relationship, although I had never seen them out together, and Tammy had never mentioned this.

I told them I'd just walk out to the highway and get a ride to town, then I could come back with the rescue crew. Well, all three of them, including Tammy, went berserk. They were yelling and screaming, kicking and pulling, grunting and groaning; and, of course, nothing worked. They made me try everything: lifting my truck, pushing it off the car, prying the car doors open with a tire tool, and even beating on the sides in the hope I could break off a piece. They were jammed between the seat and dash, and the ceiling was too close to allow them to move.

After an hour or so they agreed there was no choice but to get help. I walked about 100 yards to the highway. At the bridge I caught a ride with a trucker and went into town. Thirty minutes after I left, I was back with the rescue squad and a wrecker. Of course, they had to call the state patrol as well. Even though I said everyone was O.K., they sent for an ambulance and the firemen.

I thought everyone was real nice and pleasant, but Tammy, her mother, and Mr. Russell barely said a word to anybody. Even though Mrs. Alberson and Mr. Russell were fine, Tammy insisted on riding in the ambulance with her mother.

Before Tammy left, I tried to go ahead and give her my class ring, but she wouldn't take it. When I asked what was wrong, she just said, "Oh shut up, Bubba." Then she was gone.

Well, I understand Ricky must have heard something from Frog and Red, and I know he was getting revenge on me. He *will* pay for that. After they moved the car and truck, I understood that I hit a tree root that bounced my car's front end in the air right before I came down on Mr. Russell's car. I can understand Mr. Russell being upset about his car; I wasn't too thrilled about my truck either.

What I can't understand is why Tammy, her mom, and Mr. Russell were so mad at me. Like I said, this deal wasn't much of a secret. Anyway, as near as I can figure, it's like this: It was O.K. for the two of them to be seeing each other. It was even O.K. for people to know about them. The problem came when our little accident forced everybody to admit they knew what was going on. I suppose it's sort of like crooked politicians. Most of the time you know when one is crooked, but as long as he doesn't mess up in public where everybody has to admit he's a crook, everything is fine. Then, when he does mess up, they treat whoever reports him as if the guy doing the reporting is the real crook.

I remember seeing a movie or something one time where an old black man said, "It's a messed-up world, ain't it?" I'm beginning to understand how right he was.

The Betrayers

He awoke with a start when the rays of the morning sun crept over the rooftops and shone on his face, a face still streaked by the tears of his agony. For a moment he was blessedly confused, not sure where he was or how he had gotten there. Quickly, he recognized his surroundings. Only a couple of hours earlier he had stumbled into this Jerusalem alley where he had sunk to the ground; his head buried in his arms as they in turn rested on his drawn-up knees. In fact, his robe was still damp at the knees—a testament to the volume of his tears.

As the light's intensity increased, Peter covered his face with his hands. The darkness brought back memories of the night before—the soldiers, led by Judas, coming to arrest Jesus in the garden; the mob taking Jesus to Caiaphas; the people who had recognized Peter as a follower of Jesus; the denials of that association and the bitter pain that followed. The pain had driven him through the streets the night before—the pain of his weakness, fear, and sin. Even worse was the fact that Jesus had seen the weakness in him; he had predicted the denials. Peter sighed as he wondered how he would face his beloved Jesus. Then he wondered if he ever again would face Jesus. Then he noted a feeling that he was not alone, that he was being watched.

His head snapped to the left as he hurriedly scanned the alley. As his eyes adjusted from full sun to the shadows, he began to make out a form. Someone was crouched among some water pots and baskets that had been stored under a stairway. As Peter shifted, the head turned, and a shaft of sunlight fell upon a pair of eyes. The eyes blinked, and Peter knew the identity of the figure. His soft cry of recognition caused the eyes to widen in terror.

"Judas, you son of wickedness!" Peter cried as he scrambled to his feet. He ran to the stairway, drawing his sword as he went. "Come out, the darkness cannot cover you now!"

When Judas made no move, Peter swung his sword twice, cutting through baskets and shattering clay pots until nothing separated him from the cowering figure. "Yes, yes," Judas sobbed, "kill me, run me through with your sword, and grant me the mercy of death." Peter tensed, raised his sword above his head, but found himself unable to strike. As Peter stood there, frozen, Judas peeked out from his arms with which he had covered his face.

"Go ahead!" hissed Judas, "strike me; only make sure it's my neck and not my ear as you did with Malchus in the garden." For a moment, Peter continued to stare with utter hatred at Judas, but slowly he lowered his sword. The only sounds were the muffled sobs and sniffles of Judas, still crouching among the jagged pieces of clay and crumpled mass of reeds. Peter turned his back to Judas and hung his head.

"I . . . I thought you were . . . going to . . . kill . . . me," Judas mumbled after a while.

"I was . . . but I can't," said Peter in a soft voice, his back still toward the shadowy figure. "Why, Judas? Why did you do it? What could you have been thinking? Did you secretly hate him? I . . . I don't understand."

"Nor do I. Everything seemed so clear last night, but not anymore," Judas replied. "Anyway, I don't guess it matters now. I understand Jesus is to be condemned. I feel I have been as well."

"Yes, I guess you would," said Peter, the anger still not completely absent from his voice.

"I . . . I don't suppose there is anything that can be done?" asked Judas hesitantly.

"No . . . nothing," whispered Peter as he turned to face Judas.

Judas allowed his eyes to meet Peter's for only an instant before bowing his head and mumbling, "He knew, you know."

Peter was not sure he had heard correctly. "What was that?" he asked.

"He knew," Judas said plainly.

Peter was silent, thinking Judas was referring to Jesus' foretelling of the denials. Then Judas continued: "He said at the Passover meal that someone would betray him. Remember how everyone asked who would do such a thing. He identified me. That was when I left. I knew if I didn't go, then I would be unable to do as I had promised."

"How noble of you to honor your promise," sneered Peter. The remark created an uneasy silence for several moments until Peter spoke again. "Ah, Judas, I have no right to criticize you, though. In my own way I have betrayed him as well."

"No, Peter, once the mob arrived with me there was nothing you could have done to save him."

"No, but I could have had the courage to stand by him. Last night people accused me of being one of his followers, and every single time I denied it. I even threw in a few oaths and curses to drive home my point."

"Oh," said Judas softly, and then, "I guess none of us is as smart or brave or . . . faithful as we like to think we are."

"No . . . we certainly are not," said Peter.

Slowly and shakily, Judas tried to rise to his feet. Instinctively, Peter reached out, took Judas by the hand, and assisted him. For a moment they stood, hands clasped, each looking into the eyes of the other before Judas broke the gaze. "I should . . . uh . . . should go," he said, turning from Peter to lean against the stairway.

"Wait!" Peter blurted, "Judas, don't go off like this. Come back with me."

"Back where?"

"Well, I'm not sure. I thought maybe I would try to find some of the others. They may have gone back to the house where we ate the Passover meal."

This time, Judas sneered, "Yes, I am sure they are all most anxious to see me."

Peter stepped up behind Judas and placed his hand on his friend's shoulder, "You need not fear them; they're not all hotheads like me."

"I know," Judas replied, glancing back at Peter. "Besides, it's not the others that I fear; it's Jesus."

"Jesus?" Peter asked.

Judas was growing impatient and even more self-conscious now. "Yes, Jesus. I have betrayed him, Peter. I just want to leave —to get away—for good. I don't even want to know what happens now."

Sensing the urgency in Judas' voice, Peter began to plead more desperately. "No, Judas, you need not fear Jesus either. I know how you must feel, but it will be O.K."

"You know how I feel!" exclaimed Judas, whirling to face Peter. "You? Do you know what it is like to have sealed the death sentence of one you followed for three years? Do you know the chill I felt in my soul when he sat there at the meal and told me what I had planned to do? Do you know how agonizingly heavy these filthy coins in my pouch must feel? Do you?!"

"Yes, yes!" Peter screamed in reply. "That's what I've been trying to tell you. He also predicted my denials. He told me I would deny knowing him, and I passed it off like it was nothing. Then when I was challenged as one of his followers, I passed off my relationship with him as if it were nothing. But I'm going back, Judas. I'm going to find him and gather the others together. Wherever they take him, we will be with him. Perhaps we can do nothing, but we will not stop following him. I am convinced of his love even for betrayers like . . . well . . . like you and me. Come back with me, Judas. I know he will forgive you."

"What makes you so sure of that?" Judas asked. There was a hesitancy in his voice, the hesitancy of one who wants to know something and yet at the same time is terribly afraid of knowing.

Peter thought for a moment before replying. He sensed the need to choose his words carefully. "I am not sure it is any one thing, Judas. I know that these last three years I have heard him speak over and over about the importance of forgiveness. I remember him telling us to love not just our friends but our enemies as well. I remember him taking time to talk to people that most Jews despise.

"And I keep thinking about last night—the things he said to us, the way he acted. I think he sensed or somehow knew what would happen. I'm sure he did know of your plans, just as he knew I would deny him. But he did nothing to alter the course of events, Judas. Don't you think he could have done something had he wanted a different outcome?"

"I don't know, Peter. All I do know is that I am more afraid than I have ever been in my life," said Judas as he sagged back against the stairway.

This time as Peter spoke, there was genuine tenderness in his voice: "I, too, am afraid. I am afraid of the part of me that I discovered last night—the part that Jesus saw all along. I am afraid of what lies ahead for Jesus. I am afraid that I might not see him again. But, most of all, I am afraid that I will see him, and this time we will both know how weak and sinful I am. But I am counting on something. I am counting on his message of love and grace, and I believe that he will show his love and grace to me. I have to believe that, Judas; and I want you to believe it as well."

"Oh, how I wish I could, Peter; how I wish I could."

"You can, Judas. We are all betrayers in one form or another. We are all sinners, but Jesus' grace is more powerful than our sin. That's what it boils down to—being willing to admit that he is stronger. I . . . I guess it's kind of like a surrender to him."

Judas sighed deeply and said, "Peter, you make a lot of sense; but to be honest, that, too, scares me. I guess I have a difficult time surrendering, even to something as wonderful as grace. I've always been pretty self-sufficient and sure of myself—until now. Now . . . now I don't know what to do."

"Come with me," Peter began.

Judas cut him off, saying, "No . . . not now, anyway. Maybe later, I uh . . . I have something I need to do," he said as he fingered the bag of money in his pouch. "You go ahead, Peter. Maybe I'll catch up with you later."

Judas walked out of the alley into the full sunlight with Peter behind him. Judas turned one way, and Peter turned the other way. After a few steps, Peter paused to look over his shoulder. Judas was making a purchase from a passerby. Peter saw that the purchase was a length of stout rope.

A Simple
Little Tree

Like most families, Christmas for our family was a special time of year, a time in which each member became involved in decorating and preparing for the season. In fact, we followed an almost ritualistic routine.

The routine actually began in mid-November. My grandfather and I went hunting on Saturdays during the fall. While out in the fields, we searched the fence lines and woods for a suitable cedar tree. For two years my grandfather used an artificial tree, but as he put it, "The smell of aluminum does not do much to promote the Christmas spirit." It seems we were always able to find a tall, full cedar with just the right shape. A couple of weeks before Christmas, then, we cut the tree and brought it to the house.

My father was not a hunter, but he always went with me and my grandfather to cut the tree. It invariably took the entire morning to get the tree home because this day was the one time each year that the three of us were out together. In a very real sense, I guess my father instigated the spirit of the season in each of us. He was one of those individuals who, even as an adult, was able to retain an almost child-like sense of anticipation and excitement with regard to Christmas.

After cutting the tree in the morning, we spent the afternoon putting it in the stand, getting out the decorations, and checking the strings of lights. Finally, after supper, it was time to decorate. Each of us had a role to play in the process. I decorated most of the tree, with my father taking care of the portion that was out of my reach. My grandfather supervised the work and teased me, saying that when I finished he could barely see the tree for the ornaments, tinsel, and lights. My mother and grandmother usually chose to try and stay out of our way, using the time to collect cedar we trimmed for use on the front door.

The next afternoon my grandmother and mother formed a wreath out of cedar, pine boughs, or holly sprigs to be hung on the door. Other greenery, surrounding a large white and gold candle, went on the mantle in the living room. Candles were placed in the house along with a manger scene, a table arrangement, and my favorite decoration: a bank in the form of Santa Claus asleep in a chair.

On Christmas morning my Dad invariably awakened before I did in order to start the fire in the living room and to make sure all was in order. My mother was not an early riser, and it took some time for my Dad to coax her into the living room. Finally, with everyone present, we opened the gifts.

My grandmother always prepared Christmas dinner and invited a couple of aunts and uncles to join us. The entire day was a day for the family to be together and enjoy the beauty and fellowship of the season.

This tradition continued at our house until 1970 when I was fifteen years-old. My father died in the spring of the year of a sudden, massive, coronary attack. As I look back on the time, in a sense, I am not sure our family had recovered from the shock by December.

We went through the motions of our Christmas ritual as we always had, and yet the spirit was not quite the same. I remember consciously trying to take the place of my father but not succeeding. The decorations were the same, just as elaborate as they had always been—perhaps even more so. Maybe we unconsciously attempted to fill the void left by my father's death, but things were not quite the same and over the next few years only grew worse. We seemed to forget to use one or two traditional decorations each year. Perhaps the lowest point was the Christmas six years after my father's death. I shall always remember it as the one when the spirit of Christmas almost disappeared from our house.

When I arrived home from college, no decorations were out. My grandfather stopped hunting the year before, so there was no tree. The year before, my grandmother had gotten out the decorations and had my grandfather cut the one cedar tree out of our backyard. This year, however, she had broken her leg and was in a cast. It did not take long to realize there were no plans to decorate for Christmas.

At first the change did not really bother me. We had come to this point gradually over the past six years, so it was not all that surprising. In a sense, perhaps we had expected the change. As

Christmas drew near, however, I found myself longing as never before for the spirit of the years before my father died. I began to realize just how empty the house really was. The elaborate decorations were still in the attic, and yet no one would even suggest bringing them down. After all, there was no tree. The cutting of the tree by my father had always begun the ritualistic chain of events that led to our house being literally filled with the symbols of the season, and so it seemed there was no need to decorate.

On 23 December I was next door at my aunt's house when my grandfather came over. At one point he found himself alone in my aunt's den looking at her Christmas tree. I saw him gently touch the boughs and ornaments, almost caressing each one until he found himself staring at the star on top. I thought he would stand there staring at the star for an eternity. Finally, he glanced out the window at our house, sighed, and left. Seeing my grandfather like that was just too much for me. I, too, left and went walking in the small patch of woods behind our house. Lost in my thoughts, I kept walking until I was almost on the verge of tears.

I remember closing my eyes and leaning against a tree. In part, I was sharing the disappointment of my grandfather; in part, I was grieving over two deaths—the death of my father and the death of the Christmas season at our house.

Oh, I know there should be more to Christmas than trees, candles, and other decorations. I know the true spirit should be found in the celebration of the birth of the Christ. In fact, we never lost that. We drove by the live manger scene at the Baptist church, attended the services, and experienced the spirit of the season at church. But family and tradition are powerful forces; and with part of the family and all of the tradition missing, the void that was left was immense.

When I opened my eyes, they took a moment to focus through the salty fluid that had formed lenses over them. As they cleared and as I looked around, however, I saw a tiny cedar tree no more than three feet high. I had never seen a cedar tree in this patch of woods before. It was surprisingly full for its size and possessed a beautiful conical shape. Almost without thinking, I ran over and pulled the little tree out of the ground, roots and all. I turned to start toward the house, but stopped.

Thoughts raced through my mind as I stood there holding the little tree: "We are only two days away from Christmas. Why bother with this now? Mother will not want to go through the clutter of the attic to get the decorations out. The tree may even be too small for ornaments."

In anger and frustration, I turned and threw the tree as far as I could. It twisted and turned until it bounced off the trunk of another tree and collapsed among the leaves on the ground. As I looked at it, I almost began to grieve for the tree as well. I became angry at myself for pulling it out of the ground. I walked over to try to replant it, but for some reason I do not yet understand, I changed my mind again. I took the little tree home with me.

As quietly and quickly as possible, I found a flower pot, filled it with dirt, and placed the little tree in it. Without saying a word to anyone, I put the tree on a stool in front of a window that faced my aunt's house next door. The moment of truth arrived quickly as my mother entered the room with a stern, "What is that?"

"It's a Christmas tree," I said, deciding to forego any explanation or plea. I expected to hear how small it was, how the limbs would bend under the weight of the ornaments until the ornaments slid off, how much trouble it would be to get the ornaments out, and how it was already two days before Christmas.

Instead, there was a long pause as my mother stared at the tree. I stood by, afraid to break the silence. Finally, in a soft and tender voice, my mother said, "There are some tiny Christmas balls around here somewhere. I wonder if we can find them."

Things happened quickly then. I climbed to the attic and, following my mother's instructions, located a box of cherry-tomato-sized green, gold, and red balls. They were practically unused and shown radiantly in the light. As we put them on the tree, my grandmother entered the room. Without saying a word she disappeared, returning a few minutes later with a small string of miniature lights that in years past had framed the front door to highlight our wreaths. A small angel that had hung from the limbs of the larger trees was just the right size to secure to the top of the little tree. With the angel in place, the tree was complete. As my mother turned off the lamp, I plugged in the small string of lights.

The little tree was beautiful. It was much smaller than any tree we had had before, and it was not completely covered with ornaments as the larger trees had been. We could actually see the branches stretching out like tiny arms covered with an intricate design of dark green lace that was dotted with shining sequins and red, green, and amber jewels. We stared in silence.

My grandfather began opening the door to the room, grumbling, "Why in the world did you have to have those lights?" Then he stood still and silent as he saw the little tree.

In the glow of the miniature lights I saw my grandmother smile. Through the glint of the suppressed tears in her eyes, I saw my mother smile. Then, I heard a faint chuckle from my grandfather as he turned to leave the room.

"Where are you going?" I asked.

"To the phone," he said, "I'm going to call next door and tell them to look out the window at our Christmas tree." I felt tears warming my own eyes as the sight of the tree and the memory of my father warmed my heart.

Christmas never would be the same without my father, but the spirit of Christmas could live on in our house. The huge trees, loaded with ornaments, and the elaborate decorations would never again have the same meaning. In the quiet beauty of a simple little tree, the spirit of the season was revived.

As we celebrate the birth of the Christ, let us remember that this event took place not in a large, elaborately decorated building, but rather in a simple little stable. May the simple beauty of Christ's birth warm our souls, just as the simple little tree warmed the hearts of my family that Christmas.

Christmas
with Gramps

"How long will we have to stay, Dad?" The question was one that I had both expected and dreaded at the same time and one that I feared would be a portent of things to come. To his credit, Eric resisted asking the question for the two hours of the trip. As we entered the town where I grew up, however, my fifteen year-old son's patience was exhausted.

"We're just going to spend the day," I responded, understanding Eric's feelings and yet wanting to complete the rest of the trip in silence. Nostalgia occupied my thoughts as my eyes took in the sights of a small-town main street that had hardly changed in more than two decades. Though I knew it was impossible, I actually wondered if the red and white candy canes affixed to the street lamps and the dark green garland that stretched from store to store were not the same decorations that were used when I celebrated Christmas as a child in the town.

The store owners continued to decorate their windows each year for a Christmas contest that Mr. Harling's department store won each year. Of course, Mr. Harling owed his impressive streak to the fact that his brother-in-law was the local mortician. After marrying Mr. Harling's sister, some years back, Rufus Thomas helped his new bride begin the town's first and, thus far, only floral shop. Each year Mrs. Thomas took great care in decorating her brother's store-front with the best her shop could offer.

I recalled that when the Thomas' eldest son returned to practice medicine at the county hospital, people around town joked that if the younger son ever received "the call" to preach, the family might face anti-trust charges. As fate would have it, the younger Thomas boy was called instead to own and operate Bubba's Blue Moon—a combination pool hall, beer joint, and bait shop that anchored the same corner at the edge of downtown as long as I could remember. Now we turned at that corner onto the street of my childhood home.

As we traveled the last three blocks to our destination, the unique silence that resulted from tension and apprehension settled over our entire family. Turning into my father's driveway, I noted the blinking lights in the living room window and the absence of any type of decoration on the front door. Until my mother's death two years ago, a large pine wreath accented by a red and green bow had hung on the door each Christmas.

"Let's get the food," said Joanne. The food was a virtual feast my wife had spent all Christmas Eve preparing. Eric grabbed the turkey, Joanne carried the pan of dressing, and Christi—our thirteen-year-old daughter—somehow balanced fruit cake and sweet potato pie on top of a casserole dish filled with creamed corn. As I loaded a tray with beans, cranberry sauce, a relish tray, and bread, three-year-old Lisa began to stir in her car seat.

"Daddy, I want to get out!" Lisa moaned. "O.K., Hon," I said as I placed the tray on top of the car and began to unbuckle her. Born one December ten years after what we thought would be our last child, Joanne and I called Lisa our biggest Christmas surprise, but she was also our best. With Eric and Christi at the age where social status is heavily dependent upon one's ability to project indifference, Lisa's energy and enthusiasm for life provided a refreshing balance.

Gramps, as the children called him, greeted us at the door with a soft "Merry Christmas," a trace of a smile, and a light stiff hug—for everyone that is but Lisa, whose back he patted as she clamped her arms around his neck.

"It's good to see you, Dad," I said.

"Good to see you too, Pete," he said. "You can go ahead and put the food on the table. I'm afraid the candle and holly sprigs are about all I could come up with for decoration."

"But they're perfect, Gramps," said Joanne. "Come on and sit down. I know you must be hungry."

"I sure am," said Eric, which came as no surprise to any of us.

As we took our seats around the table, I asked Gramps if he wanted to return thanks. As usual he declined. After the prayer, the only sound was that of flatware making contact with china and occasional small talk. A year or so ago such quiet put each of us on edge, but by now it had become the expected routine.

If my mother had been there, things would have been much different. Even Eric and Christi would have been drawn out of their indifference if Mother had been there to question and tease and tell them how big they were getting. But Mother was gone, and Gramps, who had always been somewhat quiet and withdrawn, seemed to have retreated even further into his shell. I had some understanding of my father, but not the depth of perception of my mother.

I always wondered if my father ever felt over-powered by my mother's personality, though he was not one of whom you asked such questions. Once, when I questioned my mother concerning this, she merely smiled and said, "Your father is a man of what you might call quiet strength. One day you'll understand him a bit better and realize that strength is not always readily apparent."

As we finished eating, Joanne and Christi began to clear the table. Gramps rose to help but was quickly shooed into the den with Eric, Lisa, and myself as Joanne and Christi headed for the kitchen to complete the clean-up.

"Daddy, when are we going to open presents," Lisa asked somewhat impatiently.

"In a little while, Hon," I said as I crossed the room to Gramp's gun case. "Did you sell your twenty-gauge?" I asked.

"Yea, since I stopped hunting I figured I'd keep just the sixteen gauge, the over-under twelve, and the rifle. They could be worth something one day."

"I think I'll step out and get the gifts from the car," said Eric. I understood his discomfort. Hunting was the greatest barrier between Eric and Gramps. I went hunting with Gramps in spite of the fact that I was never particularly at ease with guns. Eric, however, plainly told Gramps that guns scared him and that shooting things made him feel bad. Secretly, I admired his frankness and was relieved that I would not have to bother with deciding when Eric would be old enough to "get his own gun."

"Daddy, let's go look at the tree," pleaded Lisa.

"Well, why don't you ask Gramps if he wants to go in the living room with us," I said.

"Do ya'?" Lisa asked as she spun around excitedly.

"No, no, y'all go ahead," mumbled Gramps as he reached for a newspaper that lay beside his chair.

I had long since made the decision not to beg Gramps to take part in things with the family. "That's just his 'way'," my mother always said when he withdrew from us. Often Mother would eventually manage to involve my dad in what we were doing. I, however, never managed to learn the secret from her.

The Christmas tree was no more than five feet tall, but was very pretty. I actually got more joy out of Lisa's reaction to the tree than anything else. Squeals signaled her discovery of each ornament. The ornaments were not like the ones we used at our house. They were ancient ones from my childhood: hand-carved, brightly painted wooden figures; striped balls of glass; and styrofoam balls covered with fabric, ribbon, beads, and glitter that were made on cold December nights as my mother and I sat in the cozy warmth of the den watching the T.V. Christmas shows of Andy Williams, Perry Como, and Tennessee Ernie Ford.

My father often worked late on those nights. Extra money at Christmas was always welcomed. Even after he quit work, my mother said that because of his work he had trouble joining all of us during Christmas celebrations. I never quite understood but, as mother was quick to point out, I never had to work like he did.

As Joanne, Christi, and Eric gathered with Lisa and me, we began to sift through the presents. "Pete, shouldn't you get Gramps in here?" Joanne asked.

The question irritated me. My reply of, "Would you like to tell me how?" was much too curt. I called into the den, "Gramps we're about to open presents; come on in."

"You go ahead, I'll be there in a bit," he said.

Lisa immediately did as her grandfather suggested and ripped into the biggest box she could find. Luckily it was for her. Soon we were surrounded by a sea of toys, sweaters, books, paper, boxes, and ribbon. Christi and Eric moaned as they saw the boxes from their great aunt. Aunt Millie always gave them underwear. This year was no exception.

"Dad," Christi sighed, "I don't mean to seem ungrateful but why does Aunt Millie do this?"

"I've told you before honey, I don't know," I said suppressing a smile. "I felt the same way as a teenager when she did that to me. But hang in there; now that I'm an adult she gives me a card with money in it. The money is mine to do with as I please. I can buy anything I want with that money—no questions asked."

"I can hardly wait," said Christi, a tinge of hope in her voice. "What did you do with your money last year Dad?"

"I bought underwear," I stated proudly just before ducking a couple of boxes.

Finally, as the last of the boxes was unwrapped and as Lisa was quickly wearing out a battery-operated puppy from Christi and Eric, Gramps wandered into the room.

"Here you are, Gramps," said Joanne with a smile that would have melted anyone else.

"Thanks," mumbled Gramps as he removed the green bow. After fumbling with the paper and finally lifting off the top, he pulled out the dark gray hat that we had spent days trying to find.

There was genuine excitement in Joanne's voice as she explained, "It was the kid's idea. They thought you might like a new one, and this one seemed perfect since gray is your favorite color."

Gramps, at times, wore a hat even while sitting in his favorite chair reading the paper. His current chapeau was a stained, brown, shapeless mass that had long since seen better days.

My father's response to this gift our family had so carefully and excitedly chosen was the last straw as far as I was concerned. He looked at the gift, turned it over in his hands, and mumbled, "Thanks." Once again he headed back for the den. Evidently I was the only one who heard him say to himself as he left the room, "I've already got a hat. Nothing wrong with my hat."

I couldn't bring myself to stay to open the gift from Gramps. It did not matter; it was always one envelope with a check for each member of the family. Perhaps I was ungrateful, but the practice always seemed to me to be a way of avoiding the trouble of choosing a gift for any of us—sort of taking the easy way out. Joanne and I received money from other family members, but even Aunt Millie took the care to find out the size underwear the kids wore. Actually I was being unfair; but the day, characterized by the then familiar routine, had brought to the surface the frustrations concerning my father that had been building for years.

I left the living room and went to stand on the back porch where I longed for the reconciling presence of my mother. She could have handled Gramps. She could have made the day the joyful experience it was supposed to have been.

Quietly entering the kitchen, I crossed to the corner where I could stand and look at my father as he sat in his chair reading his paper, his head topped by that grotesque blob of a brown hat with which he could find no wrong. Gramps did not see me as I stared at him from over his left shoulder. As I watched him, I wondered if I should confront him about his attitude—tell him about his knack for putting a damper on everything—tell him it would not kill him to reach out to his grandchildren and get to know them. Or perhaps I should just let it go and accept that what had not changed for as long as I could remember would never change.

The incident happened rather quickly, but I finally understood something vitally important about my father. Lisa went slowly into the den, yawning and rubbing her eyes. The excitement of the day had finally caught up with her, She was tired and sleepy. Gramps did not see her; his vision was blocked by the newspaper.

"Need a lap, Gramps," Lisa said with a yawn. Then, before her grandfather could even move the paper, the three-year-old had crawled beneath the pages to his lap, put her head on his chest, put her arms around him, and with a sigh, fell asleep.

I held my breath as I waited for my father's reaction. Relating to Eric had been difficult for him, and with Christi he had no idea where to begin. What would he do with Lisa? I have no idea what I expected, but I would never have expected what I witnessed.

For a moment, Gramps sat motionless; then slowly and gently, he folded the paper and placed it beside his chair. He began to rub and pat Lisa's back but quickly stopped—only to remove his old hat, reach down, pick up the new gray hat, and place it on his head. Then he resumed the gentle, loving pats and strokes of his peacefully sleeping granddaughter's back.

Quietly I slipped out of the kitchen to return to the back porch. There it occurred to me that we were celebrating a season in which we gave thanks for the gift of another child—a child who also touched people by reaffirming their worth and reaching out to them with unconditional love. May your Christmas be as happy, as satisfying, and as meaningful as that Christmas was for me and my family.

The
Star
Tree

The sign read, "STARR, GEORGIA CITY LIMITS"—or at least I assumed that it did. My heart was not in the mission I was on. I had driven most of the twenty-odd miles to Starr in somewhat of a daze. Perhaps it was a survival instinct, or perhaps a blessing from God (if God was still in that kind of business) that I was able to drive in such a state of mind.

I visited Starr at the insistence of my wife. The battle we fought over this issue had been long, subtle, and quite destructive. But, at last, I gave in—deciding that pain was pain, and perhaps I would simply be trading one pain for another. Lately, there did not seem to be any way of escaping pain—no place to hide, no place to run, no way to fight.

Of course, when I agreed to do what she was asking, I thought she would come with me. So, earlier, when she begged off, saying she could not make herself go—that it would be too upsetting—I wanted to grab her shoulders and shake her and ask how the hell she thought I felt. Of course, I did not. I simply climbed into the car and drove off without saying a word. As I glanced in the rear-view mirror at her standing beside the mailbox, I knew she would have preferred that I had shaken her.

As I turned into the city hall parking lot, I saw a policeman. I called to him and, after glancing at the scrap of paper in my hand, asked how to find Doug James' office. He pointed up the steps to an entrance and said, "In there, second door on your right."

I thanked him and, after parking the car, entered the building and found the second door on the right. The glass read "DOUG JAMES—CITY CLERK." I entered and found myself in a cramped office filled with filing cabinets; filing boxes; a table with a coffee-maker and all the trappings; and a paper-littered desk, behind which sat a small, dark woman who—guessing from the name-plate on the desk—appeared to be Shandell Thomas.

"Hello," she said in a surprisingly low and husky voice.

"Hello, my name is Ben Street, and I'm supposed to see Mr. James."

Without saying a word, she rose and disappeared through a doorway. A moment later she reappeared and said, "Right this way."

I threaded my way between file boxes and the desk and through the doorway until I found myself in a larger office that was, remarkably, just as crowded as the first. In addition to the jungle of filing containers, this office contained a couch strewn with file folders and two chairs that were strangely empty. Doug James—a small, stout man with reddish-brown hair, a moustache, and wire-rimmed glasses—met me with a handshake and smile.

"Sit down, Mr. Street," he said as he motioned me to one of the chairs. He wore khaki pants, a plaid shirt, and a red tie. The shirt was short-sleeved, which struck me as oddly out of place for December—even in middle-eastern Georgia. His smile struck me wrong as well. I thought it looked fake, though I admit I was not in a very receptive mood.

"I understand you want to place a star on the tree," he said, his expression and voice tone taking on the manner of those at the funeral home. At least at the funeral home I did not get one of those false smiles.

"Well," I said, clearing my throat, "I would like to inquire about that possibility."

"Yes sir," he said, shifting nervously in his chair and appearing to re-group a bit. "The cost is fifty dollars, which pays for the star, helps with our maintenance costs, and covers the cost of the newspaper listing and the photograph we will send you. Half of the fifty, of course, goes to the veterans' office here in town as a memorial to . . . the deceased."

"The deceased"—he didn't even know who had been killed; plus, he thought my concern was only about money. I did not care much for this young man.

He must have read the expression of displeasure on my face, for he quickly stammered, "Uh well . . . you see, the uh, twenty-five dollars for the uh office helps with some of their activities—parades and things—and, well, you see they buy the flags we place downtown for the July fourth parade . . . and. . . oh, you're welcome to come to that—that is you and your uh, your family."

I was somewhat enjoying the sight of him squirming in his chair as his tie flopped from side to side, and its bright red knot bobbed as he gulped air and stuttered his spiel.

I, being very calm and assured, quietly said, as I stared directly at him, "Mr. James, the . . ."

"Doug, please," he said.

"What?" I asked in disbelief at being interrupted.

"My name—it's Doug. Please call me Doug."

"*Mr.* James," I repeated with emphasis, "the money does not concern me. Frankly, I am here only because my wife wanted this done. Our son, Benji—the 'deceased' to whom you just referred— was killed in the Persian Gulf War. Last year we didn't celebrate Christmas—didn't seem to be much point in it. I, for one, have no intention of 'celebrating' this year, but, as a concession to my wife, I agreed to check into this. Personally, I don't know that it's any better than a sideshow."

I could tell by the way he gripped the arm of his chair and shifted his weight that my last sentence had struck a nerve with him. The knowledge was most satisfying.

"I'm sorry," he said finally. "I know your loss must have been devastating."

Now, my nerve had been hit. "No, Mr. James, I don't think you know anything about my loss. Few people, thank God, do know what it's like to lose their only child. And besides, I did not come here for sympathy. I came for information."

He stared at me as though in disbelief before sighing and asking, "Well, what would you like to know?"

"There, that's better," I said, trying to manage a polite smile. "You may begin by telling me how this memorial project got started."

"Well, do you want the long version or the short version?" he asked.

"All I want is the accurate version," I replied. I was beginning to think my initial hunch had been correct. I had suspicions that this was nothing more than another money-making scheme. I am constantly amazed at how much money can be made off of the dead. The more tragic the death, the higher the stakes seem to be.

"Maybe I'd better give you the full details," he said as he rubbed his temple with his right hand and removed his glasses. "There is an elderly man in our town named Buddy Jackson. Buddy's family has been in this area for ages. He owns the John Deere dealership. For many years has served on our city council.

"Buddy's nemesis on the council in the late sixties was a man named Grayson Grant. Grayson was a northerner who moved here from Chicago after taking early retirement. It seems his wife had some relatives who lived here years ago. Both he and his wife are dead now, but when they first arrived they jumped into community activities with both feet. As you may know, that doesn't always go over well in a small southern town.

"I imagine Grayson and Buddy were destined to butt heads from the beginning. Grayson won a seat on council, and the die was cast. Maybe it was because he was from the north or, maybe, because he was used to city life. Anyway, Grayson believed in fast action and in offering incentives that he thought could attract industry to the community.

"Buddy was just the opposite. He was conservative and always suspicious of change. He felt that what was good enough for his dad and granddad was good enough for him—and, apparently, everyone else in town, too. Grayson was too pushy, and Buddy was too stubborn. So, a lot of the council's time was spent fighting the battles those two initiated.

"Once, we had a car accident where three teenagers had been drinking. All three were killed, and it hit the town hard. Buddy decided the town officials ought to make a statement. He proposed finding a wrecked car and placing it in front of one of the empty buildings on Main Street with some kind of sign. Grayson opposed the idea, saying that it would be insensitive to the families of the three kids. But Buddy had enough pull with other members of council to swing the vote. Then, to kind of rub Grayson's nose in it, he suggested that a committee that Grayson chaired be given the task of doing this. Buddy strutted for a few days after that, but it back-fired on him.

"The next week Buddy went out of town to a John Deere dealers' meeting. While he was gone, Grayson talked to Buddy's wife and convinced her to sell him Buddy's old fishing car for about twice what it was worth. The first thing Buddy saw when he returned to town was his favorite old car smashed up with a sign on it reading: 'The Tragic Result of Bad Decisions.' "

I'll admit I caught myself chuckling at that point, but I quickly recovered and asked, "Mr. James, could you please get to the point?"

"I am getting there, Ben," he said. "Buddy had five children, and they were a close family. Whenever one of his children reached his or her sixteenth birthday, he planted a fir tree in the backyard. Then, the year the child turned twenty-one, the tree was cut and used as the family's Christmas tree.

"Buddy's youngest child was Philip. Philip was drafted and sent to Viet Nam. Less than a year before his tour would have been up, he was killed in action. He was nineteen when he died. Of course, Buddy and his family took it hard. But for Buddy, the hardest part was seeing that last fir tree in his backyard. He couldn't bring himself to cut it two years later, and he rarely looked at it without getting a tear in his eye. But, five years after Philip's death, Buddy got an idea.

"That year he proposed to the town council that they put up a tree in town to honor those from the community who had given their life for their country, and he volunteered to provide the tree. He suggested that a star could be placed on the tree in memory of each soldier. Of course, he expected opposition from Grayson. In fact, he had lined up another council member to second the motion. Before the other guy could speak up, Grayson seconded it. He went on to propose that a special star be purchased for the top of the tree in memory of Philip Jackson.

"Well, of course, Buddy and everyone else on council sat there in shock. Finally, they voted to proceed, and Grayson even volunteered to help move the tree. After the meeting, Buddy went over to Grayson's house to thank him for his support. In the course of conversation, he discovered that Grayson had a brother who was killed fighting in Korea.

"Buddy took charge of ordering the decorations. When they arrived, the star for the top wasn't flat like we had expected. Instead, it was like someone had taken two stars and passed each halfway through the middle of the other. That star was to honor both Buddy's son and Grayson's brother.

"It's amazing how this tree has pulled our town together. Some of us feel that the town kind of grows along with the tree. I don't mean to be rude Ben, but this is *not* a sideshow."

I felt my face flush; the heat radiated from it and almost made me light-headed. The story had moved me, and I wasn't sure what to say. "You, uh," I began then stopped to clear my throat, "you seem to know some rather intimate details of the history." I regretted my words as soon as I had uttered them. I sounded as if I doubted him. At the very least, the remark came across as sarcastic and that had not been my intention.

The young man was gracious in his response, not showing any anger or discomfort, "This is a small southern town; everyone knows the details of the story. Besides that, Buddy Jackson is my mother's brother. Philip and I were the same age as well as cousins. In fact, he was the closest thing to a brother that I've ever had."

The words were like a blow to my stomach. The heat in my face intensified; my eyes felt as though they would melt. "I'm so sorry, so sorry. I apologize for what I said earlier. I guess you do know about loss, Doug."

"Yes, I do, Ben. I know you have to grieve when you lose someone, and you have to move on. I wouldn't dare tell you what to do, but it seems to me that you still have some grieving left to do. Can I ask you something kind of personal, Ben?"

I felt panic within myself. My hand gripped the arm of my chair. "Yes," I mumbled quietly.

He leaned toward me, placing a hand on my left forearm. "Ben, everyone handles grief in their own way, but, I wonder, have you ever cried for Benji?"

I wondered if he felt my muscles tighten as he asked the question. "No, no, I had to be strong for Sara, my wife, you see. She, well, she really took this hard." I glanced at my watch. "I do need to be going now," I said as I reached for my checkbook. "How shall I make this out?"

Doug started to say something else, then sat back, smiled, and said, "City of Starr—Star Tree Fund."

As I left town, my mind was racing. Could there be hope even after two years? Maybe. I thought of the story of the Magi—following a star. Perhaps just as the celestial star had led those first century astronomers to a birth that brought hope and healing and unity, perhaps this star in a tree in a small Georgia town could lead my wife and me out of our grief and into a re-discovery of the joy we had once known. Perhaps the star could be as much an agent of reconciliation as it was a memorial. Perhaps.

I began to notice I was having trouble focusing on the road signs, something that happened occasionally at dusk. But this was different. Then, I noticed a strange feeling on my face and a faint taste of salt on my lips. They were tears—tears of grief, tears of hope, tears of joy. The tears diffused the lights ahead of me until they were no longer white circles. They became fuzzy—like the stars in the sky, like the stars that would soon hang on the Star Tree.

The Manger Scene
First Baptist Church
Ariel, South Carolina

A couple of years ago on 23 December, I found myself in Ariel, a town of about 10,000 in the gently sculpted foothills of South Carolina. As a child I regularly visited Ariel, right before Christmas, to spend a day or so with my Aunt Sadie. One of the highlights of my visits was the night we visited the live nativity scene at the First Baptist Church of Ariel.

The nativity scene was always a thing of wonder and beauty. Real people portrayed the characters from 7:00 to 9:00 P.M. each evening for the two weeks prior to Christmas. There was a three-sided wooden structure made of logs. Inside, Mary and Joseph hovered over a wooden crib that seemed to have been made from a single log. In this wooden crib lay a life-size doll that represented Jesus.

Mary and Joseph were flanked by wooden, painted cut-outs of a donkey, a cow, three camels, and four sheep. Before the structure stood the three wise men with their gifts; over to the side, usually around a fire, were five shepherds. On top of the building, clothed in gleaming white robes, were three angels who stood beneath a gold foil star illuminated by white Christmas lights.

Ariel Baptist Church's nativity scene was the most beautiful one I have ever seen. Even Aunt Sadie, an Episcopalian who held little esteem for Baptists, thought the presentation was impressive. I remember her saying, "Once a year those Baptists discover culture and taste. Then, the day after Christmas, just like Cinderella's carriage, they turn back into pumpkins and rats."

On this particular evening in December, Aunt Sadie's death brought me back to Ariel. Her funeral was earlier in the day, and my family and I would return to our home the next morning. Bored with our motel room and with my wife and children preparing for bed, I left to drive around town for a few minutes. I knew the chances were good that I would never again return to Ariel, and I felt an urge to do something to help me retain the fond memories of this special place. Around 9:30, I found myself driving by the Baptist church. The nativity scene was no longer there. In fact, it had been gone for fifteen years or so as I remembered. My senior year of college—the last year I had come to Ariel during Christmas—the nativity scene was not there. Aunt Sadie was not sure why, and I never remembered to ask her about the mystery.

As I pulled into the parking lot to turn around, I noticed that the lights in the sanctuary were on and that the doors were open. In retrospect, I guess I was foolish to wander into a strange building at night, but something drew me through the doors. Perhaps it is true that the Lord looks after fools.

Once inside, I realized I was in the narthex, and I noticed the middle doors to the sanctuary were open. A soft, lilting, almost haunting sound of whistling wafted out of the doors. As I moved inside them, in the chancel area I saw a small, gray-haired black man. He appeared to be dusting the pulpit furniture. The man wore a flannel shirt and well-worn overalls. A gray beard encircled his face, and his movements, though slow, displayed a certain grace and fluidity.

Fearing I might startle him, I hesitated before calling out in a stage whisper, "Uh . . . uh . . . excuse me."

If he was surprised, he gave no indication as he slowly turned to look at me. "Yassuh, can I he'p ya?"

Not sure where to begin, I simply let the words tumble out as I headed up the aisle, "I'm, uh, from out of town, but I used to visit a relative here in town when I was younger . . ."

"Who dat be?" he asked as we met and shook hands.

"Sadie Marshall."

"Yassuh, I 'members Miz Sadie. 'cose she been in dat nursin' home a right long time now."

"Almost fifteen years," I said. "But, you know, the reason I came by was when I was little she and I used to come see the nativity scene at Christmas."

"Oh yeah! Dat thing was sumpin' wadn't it?" he said, his gray beard forming a snowy wreath around his deep pink lips and gleaming white teeth.

"Yes, it was," I said, unable to keep from smiling myself. "By the way, my name is Kenneth Waters."

"Good to meet ya' suh. I be Henry Freeman."

"You know, Henry, I always wondered what happened to that tradition."

Henry chuckled, "Well, you gots a little time, I be glad ta tell ya'."

"Well, I wouldn't want to hold you up."

"Naw, naw," he said, motioning for me to sit on the front pew as he sat beside me, "I's jes' 'bout finished here. I works at de' horsepital in de day and cleans up 'roun' here in de evenin's. An' I don' gets to tell dis story to folks real offen."

With those words, Henry pulled out an old briar pipe and began to light it as I settled back for what I suspected would be a good story.

"Dat manger scene been de pride o' dis church fer years 'n' years. Oh, 'hit started out simple enough. But people gots ta donatin' stuff to it. One lady give blue silk fo' Mary's costume. 'Nother give some fine wool fo' dem shepherd's robes 'n' fo' Joseph's too. Den it was satin 'n' such wid' gold brocade fo' de wise men and fancy containers fo' dey gifts.

"One year dey gots de idea dat fresh-cut pine logs didn' look 'xactly right fo' de stable. Dey started cuttin' good logs ever' year. An' not no pine stuff—dey was oak an' some hick'ry an' even some cedar; an' dey cut 'em early so's dey'd season an' look mo' realistical. Den one man cut some animals out'en two-inch-thick plywood 'n' painted 'em realistical lookin' 'n' even coated 'em wid' some water seal fo' protection. An' dat same one hollered out'en a cedar log fo' de trough what Baby Jesus slep' in.

"Den, o' 'cose one lady had ta buy dis 'spensive, realistical-looking baby-doll 'n' 'nother one bought dis fine golden star and angel robes dat was pure white silk wid' flannel linin' so's dem angels wouldn' get cold on de roof. Lotsa' money got spent on dat manger scene. Even repairin' 'n' keepin' up 'dat stuff was 'spensive. 'Cose peoples come from all over ta see dat manger scene 'n' I reckon dem folks felt good 'bout what deys had done.

"Fact is some of 'em may have felt a little too good 'bout it. Seems 'hit gots ta be mo' of a contest dan anythin' else. Like wid' Mary's robe. 'Hit got replaced ever' three or fo' years so's 'hit wouldn' wear out. Peoples seemed ta be tryin' ta out-do one 'nothers. Den dey gots ta fussin' 'bout who gone be who in de manger scene.

"Den preacher Turner come along. He wudn' 'xactly like de other preachers dey'd had 'roun' here. De church started some fund dat he'ped peoples pay bills 'n' buy groceries 'n' git pills 'n' such dat dey needed. Hadn't nobody never done nothin' like dat 'roun' here befo'.

"Preacher Turner worked with the young peoples a lot, too. Dat was diff'rent. I 'spose he liked de manger scene alright, but he didn' git as fired up 'bout it as some had. 'Dat fussin' seemed ta gets next ta him. Den one year, after he had been here 'bout fo' year' he got the young peoples together ta go a carolin'. Only 'stead 'a' goin' to dem rich ole' widder ladies in Ashley Heights, he takes 'em down to Sugar Hill wheres de po' folks stays. Had dem kids bring canned food 'n' stuff an' dey'd sing and den take food inta dem fam'lies.

"Well, when dey finished, de preacher brung 'em back here to de church. Dey had hot chawk'lit 'n' such an' looked at de manger scene. Well, suh, one thing led to 'nother an' dey gots ta talkin' 'bout what all dey had seen in dem houses. Some said as how dey noticed houses what had stoves but no fire in 'em. Others talked 'bout houses what had holes you could see right through to de outside. One of 'em 'membered a young momma 'dat had her baby in 'a' easy chair wid' a bo'ed 'crost' it cause dey wadn' no crib. Others 'membered chilluns what had ta sleep in sweaters 'n' jeans cause dey didn' have no bed clothes 'n' some fam'lies what all slep' in one bed cause dey didn' have but one blanket.

"Now, I myself don' know 'xactly what got in ta Preacher Turner an' dem kids, but next mornin' de whole manger scene was gone, 'cept fo' de ashes 'o' de shepherd boys fire. 'Pears dat after eveh'body left, preacher Turner an' de young'uns come back later. Dey tooks hit all an' dey worked all night.

"Early next mornin' dey delivered fire'wood to de five homes dey'd visited. Dey give dem angels' robes to 'de kids what didn' have no bed-clothes. Give dem woolen robes to a coupla 'a' fam'lies what could make blankets out'en 'em. Dey tied dat star to a little cedar dey cut fo' a fam'ly what didn' have no Chris'mus tree 'n' dey took dem wise men robes 'n' give 'em to some ladies what could use the cloth ta make quilts.

"Dat little trough-like cedar log de baby Jesus laid in was took an dey put sides on it, sewed Joseph's clothes up in Mary's blue silk robe fo' a mattress, an' give it to de woman dat didn' have no crib. Dey give dem fancy containers 'n' dat 'spensive doll to some chilluns fo' Chris'mus presents.

"Den dey did one 'a' de dangedest things I ever did see. Dey took dem animals an' nailed dem over de holes in peoples houses ta keep out de wind 'n' de cold. A house'll look mighty strange wid' a realistical donkey or cow on it, but hit'll be a whole lot warmer."

At this point, Henry stopped to re-light his pipe while he softly chuckled and shook his head.

"Well, what did the congregation do?" I asked, not meaning to be as impatient as I sounded.

"Well," said Henry, "somebody called de po'lice 'bout 7:30 when dey saw dat de manger scene was missin'. Preacher Turner had jus' gotten home an' crawled in bed when de po'lice called him. Dey was a right big crowd 'a' folks here when he got to de church. So he told 'em what him an' them kids had done."

"And the congregation understood?" I asked in amazement.

"Naw suh," Henry said, "what dey done was dey fired 'im."

"Fired him?" I whispered.

"Yassuh, fired de devil out 'a' 'im de next Sunday was de way Preacher Turner described it."

"What happened to him?" I asked eagerly, caught up in the story and the character who was telling the story.

"He done O.K. His wife was a nuss so she gots a job in Atlanta, an' he went back ta school an' lernt ta be one 'a' dem couns'lers. Said 'hit was de best thing could 'a' happen't to 'im."

"And the church just didn't bother with a nativ ... uh, manger scene after that?" I asked, somewhat stunned by what I had heard.

"Naw suh, not 'xactly den," Henry replied with another chuckle. "They's went right back ta buildin' hit up agin' de next year. An' 'cose dey went right back ta fussin' wid' one 'nother. Wadn' quite de same, though. Den five year or so later what dey had got blowed down in a wind storm. Lots 'a dem young peoples what worked wid' Preacher Turner was home from college and what not dat year. Dem folks talked to de others an' from den on dey did sumpin' dif'frent. Now, 'stead 'a' standin' in a manger scene ever' night fo' two weeks befo' Chris'mus, folks here gets together each 'a' those nights an' goes out 'n' takes food an' wood an' clothes to peoples houses. An' on de two weekends dey go do fixin' up on people's homes.

"Well, I'll be da . . ." I started, stopping when I realized where I was. "Henry, I guess you've seen Rev. Turner since that night if you know all of this."

"Oh, yassuh, he come by here ever' year two, three days befo' Chris'mus. Don' guess nobody but me knows 'bout dat. He pulls up out there to de side 'a' de street an' I goes out 'n' sets in de car wid' 'im."

Henry glanced behind him a second then, with a twinkle in his eye, he said, "Gener'ly he brings a little wine, an' me 'n' him drinks a cup each. We don' say too much. He jes' sets 'n' looks at where dat manger scene used ta be an' me an' him laughs 'a' bit. He says 'hit does him a lotta' good ta see what ain' there no mo'.'"

At that moment I heard a car horn. Henry chuckled and said, "Dat be Preacher Turner, now. Come on out 'n' meets 'im if ya' will."

Instinctively I glanced at my watch and realized I needed to get back to the motel. "Thanks, Henry, but I'd better go," I said. "But do something for me. Tell Reverend Turner that the empty spot on the lawn is the most beautiful Christmas decoration I have ever seen."

Christmas Eve
at Jordan's Texaco

When we first moved to Zebulon, Georgia, my wife and I thought that Zebulon was an appropriate name for a town that seemed to be at the end of the earth. But as we settled into the community, we grew to love Zebulon and the traditions that were protected by virtue of its somewhat isolated location. The three years I had spent as the associate pastor of an urban church in Atlanta had uncannily prepared me for the pastorate of Zebulon Baptist Church.

The church in Atlanta was labeled modern, and indeed it was. At the time of my graduation from seminary, such a church had great appeal for me. In time, however, I reconsidered the value of tradition and came to believe that progress should be tempered with a certain amount of adherence to tradition.

Thus, Zebulon became my classroom in the early 1970s. The lesson I needed to learn was that tradition is not synonymous with stagnation. Tradition also has a way of granting fresh insight. The retelling of the story can lead one to a depth of understanding that is not accessible to those who are always preoccupied with writing new stories. If Zebulon was my classroom, Horace Jordan was certainly one of my teachers.

Horace was a short, round, balding man of simple tastes. He owned two suits, one for summer and one for winter, which he wore to church on Sundays. The other six days found Horace in khaki work clothes and a cap, with an ever-present stub of a cigar clenched in the left corner of his mouth. I never saw Horace smoke. Instead he chewed the cigar the way others chewed toothpicks, pausing only long enough to spit out the shredded bits of tobacco that occasionally came loose.

Horace owned Jordan's Texaco, an ancestor of today's convenience store. In addition to being a "service station"—the term Horace preferred to the idiomatic "gas station"—Jordan's Texaco was also a small general store that featured food items, a bit of clothing (essentially the kind of clothes Horace wore), and a delightful collection of inexpensive and simple toys that lured to the back shelves almost as many adults as children.

Jordan's Texaco was the fabled "gathering place" for the men of Zebulon. In time, and, no doubt as the result of special indulgence, I was allowed to participate in the gathering. The nuggets of information concerning Zebulon and our church that I mined during our "gatherings" proved to be of incalculable value for my leadership of the church. At the very least, I had very brief waiting periods for the evaluation of those initiatives of mine that proved to be unwise. Bit by bit, I learned from my mistakes and, thus, was able to avoid repeating some of them.

Horace himself was responsible for many of those cherished lessons. Though not given to discourse, Horace—through anecdotes and what those less sensitive beings among us would label gossip—revealed to me the undercurrent of our church's history. Whereas the more formal history of our church—neatly typed in double-spaced lines on pages bound in a clear plastic folder—told what had happened over the years, the history I received from Horace told me why those things happened and who actually shaped the events.

One of the most prominent shapers of history, as reported by Horace, was Dr. Hollowell, who became the pastor of the church near the end of the Great Depression. The more I learned from Horace and others of this predecessor of mine, the more my respect for Dr. Hollowell grew. A Greek scholar with leadership skills that were attractive to large city churches, Dr. Hollowell was in his second prestigious pastorate when the depression hit. The insanity and inhumanity of some of his congregants' reaction to this cataclysmic event led the scholar to a spiritual catharsis. The result of the rite of purification was a search for a pastorate in a small rural community.

In Zebulon, Dr. Hollowell found his promised land. He spent the rest of his life there farming, fishing, and ministering to the people of the community. A man of such ability, intellect, and spiritual depth would be expected to have a profound and lasting impact on a church and its community; certainly such was the case in Zebulon. Many of the things that made Zebulon Baptist a unique church were the result of Dr. Hollowell's leadership.

One such distinctive, and one for which I grew increasingly grateful, was the Christmas Eve service. In Atlanta we cancelled regular church activities whenever Christmas Eve fell on Wednesday or Sunday. In Zebulon, however, I found that people planned their schedule around the 8:00 P.M. worship service. Those people included not just our own members but most of the community at large. Whether Baptist, Methodist, Presbyterian, or Church of God, Christmas Eve at Zebulon Baptist was a tradition for most families. As the years went on, I realized that for a few people in town their only church attendance for the year was at our Christmas Eve service. In fact, about the only person in town who did not attend the service was Horace.

I knew I should not take Horace's absence as a personal affront. Nevertheless, I felt my concern about the situation was well justified. Not only did Horace miss the service but, in addition, each Christmas Eve he kept his gas station open until midnight—the only business in town to do so. In an age when the celebration of Christ's birth had become grossly commercialized and secularized, I felt the statement made by those who chose to worship God on Christmas Eve was one that deserved the respect of all, even if they did refuse to participate.

At first I chose to deal with the problem with a pastoral care approach. "Missed seeing you with your family Tuesday night; I hope you weren't sick," I said the first year.

"Well, thanks Preacher, but I've been doin' jus' fine," Horace returned with a smile.

The next year, with more knowledge of the situation, I took on the role of encourager. A few days before Christmas I made it a point to mention each time I saw Horace that I hoped to see him at church for the Christmas Eve service. Usually he responded with a preoccupied, "Uh-huh."

When Horace again failed to attend, I regrettably resorted to sarcasm. "Make much money Wednesday night?" I asked the Sunday after Christmas. Whether my smile and handshake were enough to disguise the tone of my pointed question I do not know. All I do know is that Horace's reply of "Naw, Preacher, hardly made a thang" was devoid of anger, hurt, remorse, or shame—any one of which I would have expected and had secretly desired.

By the third year I had categorized Horace's attitude as an example of the stubbornness that is one of the negative aspects of tradition. I realized Horace probably lost money by staying open on Christmas Eve, and, yet, neither devotion to God nor proven economic principles would sway him.

The third year of my tenure in Zebulon was also the year that my family's Christmas plans were altered. Because my mother-in-law had been sick, my wife and children went to her house a couple of days before Christmas to prepare for the family gathering on Christmas Day. I planned to make the three-hour journey on Christmas morning. The weather was cold and rainy. Our church's aged heating system, already pushed to its limits, broke down the afternoon before Christmas.

After making sure the word was out that the Christmas Eve service would be cancelled, I debated whether to drive to my in-laws that night. Finally I decided the weather was too bad and that the worry my travel would cause the family simply was not worth it. After a quick supper, I decided that I could make good use of this unexpected chain of events by going over to Horace's station for the evening. I figured the company would be enjoyable and, more importantly, I might have the best opportunity yet to talk to Horace about attending future Christmas Eve services.

Although I entered the station with some apprehension, my fears were quickly dispelled. "Hello, Preacher!" Horace called from behind the counter where he sat on a stool. "What brings you out tonight?"

"Well, my family's gone, and I decided I didn't care to sit around by myself tonight, so I thought I'd keep you company," I said, realizing full well that I had stopped a bit short of telling the whole truth.

"Yea, I heard 'bout the furnace at the church," he replied with a twinkle in his eye that told me no matter what I said Horace knew what I was really doing. "If you want, I'll be glad to come over day after tomorrow and bring Clete Bussey. 'Tween the two of us we might get that thang where it'll last another month or so 'till we can decide what we're gonna do."

"I would appreciate that," I said. Then, with a sigh, I continued, "I guess we don't have much choice now but to buy a new furnace." Already I was looking for an opening that would allow me to mention Horace's absence, but about that time the door opened and through it walked Wooley.

I never knew his real name, only the name he apparently chose from the song "Wooley Bully." Wooley was a tramp of sorts. Usually he could be spotted walking to and from town with a burlap sack over his shoulder. Wooley's face was wreathed with gray hair and a gray beard. In the summer he wore only knee-length cut-offs and an unbuttoned khaki shirt. As a concession to the few store owners who would tolerate him, Wooley would pull out a dingy pair of tennis loafers before entering their establishments. His only concessions to the nasty weather of this evening were a pair of unlaced boots and a plastic poncho with a hood.

"Come on in here, Wooley. Back yo'self up to the heater there," said Horace, "You been doin' all right?"

"Yassuh, purty good, Mr. Horace," said Wooley as he positioned himself in front of the gas heater.

"Hits a bad'un out there tonight, ain't it."

"Sho' is," said Wooley.

"You know the preacher here don' cha'," Horace said, nodding in my direction.

"Right, right," said Wooley as he smiled at me.

"Wooley, I hate to see you out walking on a night like this," I stated. "Stay here as long as you will, but when you get ready I can give you a ride somewhere."

" 'Preciate it Revund, but ain't no need for worry. I'll makes it all right."

I wanted to insist, but Wooley's subtle mannerisms suggested embarrassment, and Horace's slight head shake confirmed that this was a subject best dropped. After three years Horace still had lessons to teach me.

"You men want some coffee?" Horace asked as he reached for a pot he had on a warmer.

"That'd be good," Wooley said and I agreed as we moved over to take the styrofoam cups Horace had begun filling.

"By the way, Wooley," Horace began, "I found somethin' under the counter with yo' name on it." With that Horace pulled out a package wrapped in tissue paper with a red bow on it. "Santy

Claus must've known you'd be stoppin' by," he finished with a smile as he removed his cigar stub to take a sip of coffee.

"Thanky, Mr. Horace," Wooley said with a chuckle as he groped in his sack before pulling out a small dog carved from a piece of wood. I immediately noted its similarities to the other wood carvings that Horace kept on a shelf behind his cash register.

"Mighty kind of you, Wooley, and good work, too," Horace responded as Wooley offered him the carving.

By this time, Wooley had opened his package to reveal a brand new, long sleeve, khaki shirt identical to the one Horace was wearing and most likely identical to what his own shirt had looked like before he cut off the sleeves in the summer. "Oh, Mr. Horace, I sho' can use this," Wooley said as he examined the shirt.

"Yea, that Santy is somethin' else ain't he," Horace said to deflect the sentiment that had obviously made him uncomfortable.

Wooley quickly took off his old shirt, stuffed it in his bag, and carefully donned the gift—taking the time one takes to ease into a hot bath before being enveloped in its soothing heat. "Jus' right," he said. Then, finishing his coffee, he started for the door. " 'Spose I best be gettin' on. Merry Christmas to you mens."

"Merry Christmas to you, Wooley," Horace and I called.

As soon as the door closed, I turned to Horace and laughed as I said, "You old rascal, you."

"Whut?" he said, feigning innocence and quickly turning to fiddle with the packs of cigarettes on the wall behind him. I knew this to be a signal that Horace was getting embarrassed, and I knew him well enough to realize that, as had been the case with Wooley, this was a subject that needed to be dropped.

At that point Horace took from the shelf that held Wooley's carvings a dog-eared, pocket-size copy of the New Testament and Psalms. Initially I thought the move was Horace's way of making sure we changed the subject. Only later did I come to see that the story he told was his own gracious way of giving me an explanation I did not deserve in the first place.

"You ever use one of these thangs, Preacher," he began as he thumbed through the pages of the small volume.

"Sometimes," I responded, thinking that I was humoring him. (I did not have sense enough to realize that he was humoring me.)

After spitting some shreds of tobacco, he continued, "I never will fergit one day when Dr. Hollowell asked me to go visitin' with him, and I took this here Testament with me. Fact of the matter was we were going to see Tim Hayes' father. Ol' man Hayes had been right sick, and the doctor had asked me to ride with him since Tim and I had been friends since childhood.

"On the way over, I noticed on the seat between us this big ol' black Bible. I mean 'hit was a thick son-of-a-gun. Now I knew the doctor didn't use that Bible in the pulpit, and I sorta' wondered why he had it then. So I pulled out this here Testament and asked him if he ever used one of these when he visited folks. He said he didn't because it wouldn't make the right impression.

"Now I tell ya', I was kinda' shocked to hear him say that. I had never figured him to be the kind that would put on a show for folks, especially by carrin' around a big ol' Bible. 'Course I didn't say anythin' at the time and neither did he.

"Well, anyways, we got to ol' man Hayes' house and got out of the car when this big ol' hound come flyin' out from under the porch growlin' and barkin' and headin' straight for Dr. Hollowell. Only the doctor didn't even flinch. He just waited 'till that dog got in range, and when it did the doctor hauled off and slapped that dog 'cross its snout with that big ol' Bible. Well suh, he didn't do the dog any harm, but I mean that hound tucked his tail 'tween his legs and was back under that porch before you could say 'Jack Rabbit.' Then the doctor turns to me an' says, 'Now see there, Horace, your little New Testament and Psalms wouldn't have made nearly the right impression on that dog.'

"Well, I don't mind tellin' you I laughed some at the time. But I always remembered that day, and one day I got up the nerve to ask him if he wadn't afraid some folks might feel that what he done with that Bible was sacerligus. And I never will fergit what he told me then. He said, 'Horace, God never said a man couldn't be practical and still be religious. Remember when Jesus and his disciples picked grain to eat on the sabbath? Jesus didn't think that was a sacrilege. Taking care of yo'self and others is good common sense; but it's also part of the example Christ set for us. And, perhaps, there are times when that is the most sacred thing you can do.' "

I feel sure the car that pulled up to the gas pumps then must have rung the bell that alerted Horace to customers, but I must admit I did not hear the ring. In fact, as Horace headed out the door, I sat staring at the fire as the meaning of his story began to sink in. I realized Horace had carefully chosen his method of revelation so as to cause me the least amount of embarrassment. His point was unmistakable, and yet he made it in such a gentle and humorous manner, there was no chance that he could have offended me. The embarrassment I did feel was quite well-deserved, but certainly not humiliating.

Over the next couple of hours, five different cars pulled in as people bought gas and coffee or simply got out to stretch and take a break from the road. Three cars contained families with children, traveling to Grandma's. One was transporting a set of grandparents to their daughter's house. The other car was driven by a young man on the way to his fiancee's home. I learned that the elderly couple and two of the families were regulars who passed through Zebulon each year on Christmas Eve. They talked of how difficult it was to find a place open on Christmas Eve and how Horace's station was both a tradition and a necessity for their trip.

A bit later, as I helped Horace put things away and prepare to close for the night, my feeble attempts to apologize were brushed aside. Finally we walked out as Horace taped an envelope containing change and his phone number to the glass door so that anyone with an emergency could call him from the pay phone.

As Horace got into his truck, I said, "Horace I enjoyed this evening, and I know now why you stay open on Christmas Eve. By the way, how long have you been doing this?"

"Oh, ever since my last year of high school when my daddy owned this place. I remember 'cause that was the year I was in the school's Christmas pageant."

"Oh yea?" I said.

"Yea," said Horace as he put the truck in gear, "I played the part of the innkeeper." He drove away, leaving me to reflect on the importance and subtlety of the final point in the evening's lesson.